Richard Pennefather Rothwell

Universal bimetallism and an international monetary

clearing house

together with a record of the world's money, statistics of gold and silver,

etc.

Richard Pennefather Rothwell

Universal bimetallism and an international monetary clearing house
together with a record of the world's money, statistics of gold and silver, etc.

ISBN/EAN: 9783744739603

Printed in Europe, USA, Canada, Australia, Japan

Cover: Foto ©ninafisch / pixelio.de

More available books at **www.hansebooks.com**

UNIVERSAL BIMETALLISM

AND

An International Monetary Clearing House,

TOGETHER WITH

A RECORD OF THE WORLD'S MONEY,

STATISTICS OF GOLD AND SILVER, Etc.

BY

RICHARD P. ROTHWELL, M.E., C.E.,

Editor of the Engineering and Mining Journal.
Ex-President American Institute of Mining Engineers.
Special Agent of the 11th United States Census on Gold and Silver,
Etc., Etc.

NEW YORK:
THE SCIENTIFIC PUBLISHING COMPANY,
1893.

CONTENTS.

PREFACE.

The failure of the Brussels Conference to evolve, or even to suggest, any plan whatever for the permanent solution of the silver problem, or for the prevention of the dangers then evidently impending and which have since in a measure materialized in a widespread financial crisis, induced the author to suggest the following "Plan for Universal Bimetallism under the control of an International Monetary Clearing House," and he published it in the *Engineering and Mining Journal*, December 3, 1892.

The immediate and enthusiastic favor which this plan for a permanent solution of the problem has received from thoughtful men in every part of the world makes it very apparent that the time has come when civilized nations should unite in submitting to the arbitrament of an international commission of experts the solution of this vital question. The industry, the prosperity, the civilization of a large part of the human race should no longer be subjected to the dangers of ignorant experimenting in finance, nor to those of a blind, tentative, and uncontrolled natural evolution towards a less barbarous system than that now in use.

As an outcome of the interest shown in the subject, and in this suggested solution of the problem, the author addressed, by invitation, a large meeting of the Reform Club in the City of New York ; and also the World's Congress of Bankers and Financiers held in Chicago in June, 1893, and has discussed it, in many of its bearings, in the editorial columns of his *Engineering and Mining Journal*.

The substance of these addresses and editorials is now presented, briefly, in the following pages, together with certain statistical data which are the foundations on which certain of the author's statements rest.

The acute financial crisis through which the United States is now passing, and the indescribable disasters which the sudden demonetization or destruction of the money value of silver, and the consequent sudden appreciation in gold, will bring, call for prompt and wise action. Can there be any more rational, any fairer or juster method of reaching a permanent solution of this question than to submit it to the arbitrament of experts representing all the interests involved?

The adoption of this, or some analogous, plan depends upon the force of public opinion. It is therefore of the highest importance that everyone who approves of it should use his influence to make it known and to bring its important provisions before those who mould the policies of nations and those who make their laws. The author invites correspondence, suggestions, and criticism.

27 Park Place, New York.　　　　　　　　　　　　　　　R. P. ROTHWELL.
JULY, 1893.

Mr. John Richards, the able editor of *Industry*, a San Francisco magazine, says:

"We think Mr. Rothwell's monetary scheme by all odds the most rational one yet presented."

Mr. Robert Bassermann, of Mannheim, Germany, says:

"Of all the propositions I have seen, I believe the plan proposed by Mr. Rothwell to be the most able and ingenious one to solve the silver question in the way the American people wish it to be solved."

The Butte, Mont., *Daily Miner* says:

"The *Engineering and Mining Journal* has been a bitter enemy of silver, but it publishes a plan for the solution of the silver problem which in many respects can be indorsed by the most ardent advocate of free coinage."

President Williams, of the Chemical National Bank of New York, says:

"The plan proposed is thoroughly good; the ratio is equitable, and its adoption would not fail to benefit all concerned. It would lend added security to the debts of the silver countries which alone should insure its adoption."

Mr. John A. Stewart, president of the United States Trust Company of New York, says:

"The plan is grand in every way, and its adoption could not fail to please the National Banks. The ratio proposed, that of Soetbeer, is just, and should commend itself to the Western silver advocates. The plan of an international clearing house is well conceived, and will meet with nothing but approval here."

Mr. Sherer, manager of the New York Clearing House, the most important financial institution in this country, says:

"I can see many advantages that would follow its adoption. Besides the settlement of the silver question, which is by far the most important, the adoption of an international money which the plan involves, would obviate the frightful waste incident upon the shipping of gold coin as well as the waste of time and money in its frequent recoinage of foreign coin."

Mr. Muhleman, cashier of the United States Sub-Treasury, says:

"The proposed plan should be welcomed as the forerunner of a new dispensation in financial affairs, pregnant with tremendous possibilities, in the direction of uniformity of standards, furnishing stability of the media, equitable throughout the world, cheapening as well as guaranteeing exchanges and freeing commerce from burdens which cannot but enhance by their expensive clumsiness the cost of commodities to the consumer."

Mr. C. H. Gosch, Anaheim, Cal., says:

"Your proposal for the solution of the silver problem is certainly an admirable piece of work, and you may say with and as a second Archimedes, 'Eureka!'"

The Hon. Alexander R. Shepherd, Batopilas, Chihuahua, Mexico, says:

"Some such plan as your clearing house will alone help out the present condition. God speed the day when the currency of the world shall be settled for all time."

Mr. Welker Given, editor of the *Times-Republican*, Marshalltown, Iowa, says:

"Your plan is the only practicable and statesmanlike solution of this great question, and the need for it becomes more and more apparent every day. I cannot resist the belief that your plan must be adopted and will take place in history as one of the great achievements of the time."

UNIVERSAL BIMETALLISM

AND

AN INTERNATIONAL MONETARY CLEARING HOUSE.

In the growing intercourse between members of the human race various substances have been used, more or less extensively, as money or measures of value for the things exchanged ; the tendency being always towards the general adoption of a single standard of value for the whole world.

As the wealth of men increased it became more and more convenient to use standards composed of rarer, and, therefore, more valuable substances. Among the materials thus selected as standards of value on account of their desirable physical properties, as well as of their comparative scarcity, were gold, silver, copper, and some other metals which at various times have had different relative values in money. While it is true that the actual amount of money or of the standard of value in existence does not limit the total value of the substances measured, still it is certain that the rarer and harder to get is the standard the more of everything else will be given for it ; for the actual purchasing power of the standard is, like that of everything else, governed by the universal law of supply and demand.

While nations had little intercourse with each other, the maintenance of different standards of value in different countries was possible and created small inconvenience, but as intercourse increases and each country has growing commercial transactions with the others, the need, not only of a common measure of value, but of an international supervision and control over the money of the world, has become very evident. So closely are the rights and duties of nations now bound together by the needs and interests of men that no one country can act for itself alone or be guided solely by what it may deem its individual benefit without regard to the effect of its action on others. Each must have a regard for the rights and even for the interests of its neighbors, just as civilization has circumscribed the liberty of the individual by the rights of others. The world is so narrow and knowledge now so wide that no nation can permanently prosper by a policy that injures its neighbors. The real welfare of each is promoted by the prosperity of all, and civilization itself is but the outcome of this enlightened selfishness.

MONETARY SYSTEMS AND APPROXIMATE STOCKS OF MONEY IN THE PRINCIPAL COUNTRIES OF THE WORLD, 1891.

Countries, and Money Systems.	Ratio of Silver to 1 of Gold — Full tender.	Ratio of Silver to 1 of Gold — Lim'td tender.	Population in Millions.	Stock of Gold. $	Stock of Silver 1=$1,000,000 — Full tender.	Stock of Silver — Lim'td tender.	Stock of Silver — Total.	Uncovered Paper. $	Gross Total. $	Percentages — Gold.	Percentages — Silver.	Percentages — Unco'd Paper.	Percentages — Total.	Per capita — Gold. $	Per capita — Silver. $	Per capita — Paper. $	Per capita — Total. $
United States, gold & silver..	15.98	14.95	65	654,000,000	498	77	575	405,790,000	1,634,790,000	40.00	35.18	24.82	15.93	10.06	8.85	6.24	25.15
United Kingdom, gold........	......	14.28	38	550,000,000	......	100	100	50,000,000	700,000,000	78.57	14.28	7.15	6.82	14.47	2.63	1.32	18.42
France, gold & silver........	15½	14.38	39	800,000,000	650	50	700	81,400,000	1,581,400,000	50.58	44.27	5.15	15.40	20.52	17.95	2.09	40.56
Germany, gold...............	15½	13.85	49.5	600,000,000	103	108	211	107,000,000	918,000,000	65.36	22.93	11.65	8.95	12.12	4.26	2.16	18.54
Belgium, gold & silver.......	15½	14.38	6.1	65,000,000	48.4	6.6	55	54,000,000	174,000,000	37.35	31.00	31.05	1.70	10.68	9.02	8.85	23.53
Italy, gold & silver..........	15½	14.38	31	93,500,000	16	34.2	50.2	163,470,000	307,270,000	30.46	18.33	53.21	2.99	3.02	1.62	5.27	9.91
Switzerland, gold & silver....	15½	14.38	3	15,000,000	11.4	3.6	15	14,000,000	44,000,000	34.09	34.09	31.82	.43	5.00	5.00	4.67	14.67
Greece, gold & silver........	15½	14.38	2.2	2,000,000	1.8	2.2	4	14,000,000	20,000,000	10.00	24.00	70.00	.19	.91	......	6.36	9.00
Spain, gold & silver.........	15½	14.38	18	40,000,000	120	38.6	158	100,000,000	298,000,000	13.42	53.02	33.56	2.39	2.22	8.78	5.50	16.58
Portugal, gold..............	15½	14.08	5	40,000,000	......	10	10	45,000,000	95,000,000	42.10	10.50	47.40	.93	8.00	2.00	9.00	19.00
Austria-Hungary, gold ...	15½	13.69	40	40,000,000	90	......	90	290,000,000	390,000,000	10.26	23.08	66.66	3.81	1.00	2.25	6.50	9.73
Netherlands, gold & silver..	15½	15	4.5	25,000,000	61.8	3.2	65	40,000,000	130,000,000	19.23	60.00	30.77	1.26	5.55	14.44	8.89	29.88
Scandinavian Union, gold..	15½	14.88	8.6	32,000,000	......	10	10	27,000,000	69,000,000	46.38	14.49	39.13	.68	3.72	1.16	3.14	8.02
Russia, silver..............	15½	15	113	250,000,000	22	38	60	500,000,000	810,000,000	30.86	7.41	61.73	7.89	2.21	.58	4.42	7.16
Turkey, gold & silver.......	15½	15	33	......	......	45	45	......	95,000,000	52.63	47.37	......	.93	1.32	1.36	......	2.88
Australia, gold.............	15½	14.28	4	100,000,000	......	7	7	......	107,000,000	93.46	6.54	......	1.06	25.00	1.75	......	26.75
Egypt, gold.................	15½	15.68	7	100,000,000	......	15	15	......	115,000,000	86.95	13.05	......	1.13	14.29	2.14	......	16.43
Mexico, silver..............	16½	......	11.6	5,000,000	50	......	50	2,000,000	57,000,000	8.77	87.72	3.51	.57	.43	4.31	.17	4.91
Central America, silver......	16½	......	3	......	.5	......	.5	2,000,000	2,500,000	......	20.00	80.00	.02	......	.17	.67	.84
South America, silver.......	16½	......	35	45,000,000	25	......	25	600,000,000	670,000,000	6.72	3.73	89.55	6.53	1.29	.71	17.14	19.14
Japan, gold & silver.........	16.18	......	40	90,000,000	50	......	50	56,000,000	196,000,000	45.92	25.51	28.57	1.91	2.25	1.25	1.40	4.90
India, silver...............	15	......	255	......	900	......	900	28,000,000	928,000,000	......	96.98	3.02	9.08	......	3.53	.11	3.64
China, silver...............	15	......	400	......	700	......	700	......	700,000,000	......	100.00	......	6.82	......	1.75	......	1.75
The Straits.................	15	......	......	......	100	......	100	......	100,600,000	......	100.00	......	.97	......	......	......	......
Canada, gold...............	15	14.95	4.5	16,000,000	......	5	5	40,000,000	61,000,000	28.23	8.20	65.57	.59	3.56	1.11	8.89	13.50
Cuba, Haiti, gold...........	15½	......	2	20,000,000	1.2	.8	2	40,000,000	62,000,000	32.28	3.23	64.51	.60	10.00	1.00	20.00	31.00
Total..................	......	......	......	3,682,900,000	3,499.1	563.6	4,002.7	2,829,660,000	10,264,960,000	......	......	......	100.00	......	......	......	100.00

THE MONEY OF THE WORLD.

The business of the civilized world is carried on with about $10,264,968,000 of money, of which, according to the Director of the United States Mint, $3,632,605,-000 is of gold ; about $4,000,000,000 is of silver, counted at its coining ratio of from 15½ to 16 to 1 with gold ; and $2,626,663,000 is of uncovered paper money, that is of paper money which represents neither gold nor silver held in reserve for its redemption.

The distribution of this money is given in the preceding table.

It seems from this that, of the world's money, the United States holds about 15.93 per cent ; France, 15.40 per cent ; Germany, 8.95 per cent ; Great Britain, 6.82 per cent ; China, 6.82 per cent ; India, 9.03 per cent ; Russia, 7.89 per cent.

It appears also that, of an estimated population of the countries mentioned, aggregating 1,218,000,000 souls, no less than 817,000,000, or 67 per cent of the whole, carry on business on the silver standard alone, while all the rest of the world use both gold and silver, though in some cases the silver is of only limited legal tender, or is used simply in subsidiary coinage.   Every decline in the value, that is in the purchasing power, of silver therefore affects injuriously every nation, while an appreciation in the value of gold would be not less harmful to the industries and commerce of the world.

Every business man knows that it is not so much the extent as it is the suddenness of changes in values which causes the utter demoralization of business and the destruction of industries.   If changes were small in amounts, and occurred only at long intervals, business would be adapted to them without disturbance or disaster, but where the market value of silver declines suddenly 20 to 30 per cent, and no one can foresee what further decline may take place nor what its extent may be, then the business of two-thirds of the world's inhabitants is utterly demoralized, while the greatly increased demand for gold, the standard money of the other one-third of the world, must necessarily bring about a rapid and very large advance in the market price of that metal, for the supply can neither be quickly nor largely augmented.   The operation of the law of supply and demand, which brings a decline in price for an undesired surplus on the market, and advances prices when there is "a famine" or insufficient supply of any article, is absolute and inflexible.   An advance in the value of the standard means a decline in the market price of everything measured by it, including wages and every product of labor, so that this inevitable sudden appreciation of gold would bring even greater distress and disaster upon the people using the gold standard than the depreciation of silver had caused to the others.

It would require a long period of depression, or financial panic, infinitely more intense than any ever yet seen, and many bitter strikes, accompanied by by poverty and desperation and a general stoppage of the wheels of commerce, before the business of the world could be adapted to the new conditions, and men would willingly accept one-half or one-third of the wages they had been accustomed to.   Who can measure the effects of a general reduction of 50 per cent in the rates of wages, or of the almost total, sudden destruction of the exchangeable value of the money of two-thirds of the inhabitants of the world?   It is because I appreciate and dread, though I cannot measure, the effects of the commercial catastrophe which every thoughtful man knows to be impending, that I seek some simple and practical solution of this fateful problem.

It would indeed be a sad and humiliating admission to make that the intelligence and civilization of the present day can devise no safe and effective means to regulate and steady the standard of values, but that we must bungle along blindly, revolutionizing industry and commerce, while experimenting in an ignorant manner with a sudden change in the world's standards of value, the effect of which no man pretends to know or can estimate, but which everyone fears will result in vast and irreparable injury to the greater part of the human race. Such a course is not only irrational, it is barbarous and wholly inconsistent with modern civilization.

When a man following his personal inclinations does that which injures his fellows, we leave to a jury the question of his rights, and the limitations which should bound the exercise of his individual liberty. When the question is between nations, modern civilization compels a submission of the case to international arbitration, which decides and declares what are the common duties and rights of mankind, which should control the actions of individual nations.

Nations recognizing the importance of greater international postal facilities have created a postal union or clearing house which has been of such benefit that it would now be deemed a relapse into barbarism to allow each nation to regulate its own postal affairs regardless of the interests of others.

In business matters it was long ago found that the establishment of clearing houses not only afforded the means of striking final balances between the manifold transactions of its members, and thus permitted dealings of almost fabulous amount with the actual handling of very small sums of money, to the immense benefit of business, but the banks in the clearing house for their mutual convenience, benefit and protection, established such a mutual supervision or control over the individual operations as prevents unsafe methods, wild "financiering," or dishonest practices. Who would revert to uncontrolled individual liberty in banking with its countless risks, inconveniences, and disasters? It needs no argument to-day to secure the endorsement of jury trials, of international arbitration, of an international postal union, or of commercial clearing houses.

The world has outgrown the barbarous monetary methods of the past, and we should apply to the regulation of international monetary transactions those rules and limitations which have been proven of inestimable advantage in commercial business and that have become indispensable in the administration of international postal matters and in the settlement of international questions affecting the rights and duties of nations.

A MONETARY CLEARING HOUSE—A SOLUTION OF THE GREAT PROBLEM.

I would suggest that "The Silver Question" with its vast and incalculable possibilities for good or ill, for the prosperity or bankruptcy of the greater part of the human race, be submitted to the arbitrament, decision, and control of an International Monetary Clearing House, or commission, composed of expert representatives of the nations, empowered and instructed by their respective governments

1st. To select a universal monetary standard.

2d. To adopt measures for securing the use of gold and silver on such a flexible ratio as will effect permanent stability in the value of the world's money.

3d. To adopt measures for facilitating international monetary transactions and for their supervision and control.

The experience of the past justifies the belief that such a body of experts, representing the interests of the civilized world, would arrive at a wiser and juster solution of the problem than could be expected from the more or less biassed legislators of any one country.

While it may be the part of wisdom to leave this International Monetary Clearing House untrammeled by other instructions than those just mentioned, leaving to its discretion the adoption of such measures as may secure the approval of a certain majority of its members, yet it will not be amiss to outline a few points that, if not embodied in the official instructions to the commission, would yet, no doubt, form a part of its duties.

I assume that the Monetary Clearing House, either under instructions or as the result of its study of the subject, and to prevent the incalculable injury that would result from a sudden change in the world's money, would adopt the principle of universal bimetallism on a flexible ratio, and would take such measures as would secure its practical establishment in all countries. I would outline some of the measures which it seems to me would best attain the objects of the Clearing House as follows :

1st. It would ascertain the amount of money, that is of gold, silver, and uncovered notes, held by each country.

2d. It would use these amounts as the basis for the proportions in which the several nations would join in the purchase, for gold, of such an amount of the silver of the silver-basis countries as would be necessary to put each on the bimetallic basis. And also as the basis of the proportions in which the nations would join in the subsequent purchase of all the gold and silver offered each year, in excess of that specifically applied for.

3d. It could issue, for the gold and silver so purchased, international certificates redeemable in gold and silver at holder's option, or possibly in gold and silver in specified proportions.

4th. It would determine from time to time what change in the value-ratio of gold and silver is called for by the changed conditions of production.

5th. It would clear every national transaction in the purchase, sale, and emission of money.

6th. It would publish frequently the transactions of the Monetary Clearing House.

The Clearing House would act through the customary channels, the mints, of the several countries, and while establishing a standard and regulating the value-ratio of gold and silver, it would not necessarily interfere with the coinage of the nations beyond regulating the relative values of the metals employed in it, though undoubtedly there would soon follow an irresistible public demand for a uniform international currency.

This Monetary Clearing House, exercising functions somewhat similar to those of a bank clearing house, would, through the means here indicated, prevent any sudden changes and fluctuations in the value of the money of the world, which changes are so disastrous in every department of industry and commerce, yet this would not prevent a natural and gradual evolution towards a single standard **for** unlimited legal tender money, should such ever become desirable.

In establishing on an absolutely stable, permanent basis the money of the whole world and in providing a universal currency, good the world over, and in exercising a salutary supervision and control over all the monetary transactions of nations, it would develop confidence everywhere and would draw out into active use the vast amounts of both gold and silver hoarded in many countries and thus bring about such an impetus to industry and investment and such a period of general prosperity as has never been dreamed of.

I have purposely avoided embodying in this plan the working details for its execution, for there will necessarily be differences of opinion on these, and their wise solution can best be reached by the commission itself. It may, however, be well to anticipate some obvious questions, and show how simply and effectively the plan could be operated.

The appointment of international arbitration commissions, with powers to decide and settle specific matters in dispute, is no new or untried thing. The members of this Monetary Clearing House would be appointed in the same manner. Since large commissions are inconvenient and expensive, and the work is always done by a few individuals, it would probably be best that each of the great nations be represented by few, perhaps only by one, two, or three commissioners, assisted by counsel ; each nation being entitled to such a number of votes as would represent, in some fair and equitable manner, its interests both as to population and money. If we assume the foregoing table to represent these interests and that each 5,000,000 of population and $25,000,000 of money be entitled to one vote, then we would have $411 + 244 = 655$ votes.

According to this the countries now using the single silver standard, including in this India, Mexico, South America, etc., would have 270 votes, while the other countries would have 385 votes. This, however, would be of little consequence, for those using the gold standard are even more interested in securing a safe bimetallism than are those using silver alone.

AMOUNT OF GOLD REQUIRED TO ESTABLISH UNIVERSAL BIMETALLISM.

The amount of money in the world is ascertained yearly with approximate accuracy by the Director of the United States Mint, and this amount seems to afford a fair and rational basis for apportioning the purchases of such silver as it may be necessary to purchase with gold, in order to put all nations on the bimetallic basis. The amount of these purchases would probably not exceed $150,-000,000. For, according to recent official statements, the requirements of India are placed at only $75,000,000 in gold to establish an effective bimetallism. The rest of the world would scarcely need as much more. The amounts that the several gold or bimetallic basis countries would therefore pay out in gold for silver to establish universal bimetallism would be approximately as follows : The United States, $32,000,000 ; France, $31,000,000 ; Great Britain, $14,000,000 ; Germany, $18,000,000.

These amounts are quite insignificant and could easily be provided by the several nations.

As this silver would be universally accepted at the ratio adopted by the commission (let us say 20 silver to 1 gold), and would be absolutely interchangeable with gold in all the money of the world, this purchase would cost *nothing*. Having thus established all nations on the bimetallic basis without cost or sacrifice, the money of the whole world would be uniform ; gold and silver would be interchangeable in every country ; the money of all would be permanently equal, and there would thereafter be no conflict in interest, and no "scramble for" either metal would then be possible.

The several nations could each year make requisition to the clearing house for what gold and silver they desired, and if the requisitions for one metal exceeded the supply, each country would get, *pro rata*, its proportion of what was available, while if there were a surplus of either metal unasked for, each country would take its proportion of it, according to its holding of money.

The Monetary Clearing House, for whose account the gold and silver was purchased by the different mints, could issue clearing house certificates based thereon, that would form an international money, with the values stated in equivalent dollars, pounds sterling, marks, and francs, so that the actual value of the certificate would be known everywhere at sight. These certificates might be made redeemable anywhere in gold or silver at holder's option, or, if presented in large amounts, they might be redeemable in gold and silver in certain proportions. Since this plan contemplates permanency, there would be neither inducement nor desire to hoard, or to use one metal in preference to the other ; in fact, for amounts for which certificates could be used, these would be universally preferred to either gold or silver, as the experience of this country with its gold and silver certificates has abundantly demonstrated. It might indeed be expected that but little of the gold or silver purchased would ever be coined or used except for small change.

The frequent publication of the transactions of the Monetary Clearing House is by no means unimportant. Since every national transaction in the purchase, sale, or emission of money must be reported to the Clearing House, the publication thereof to all the world would not only tend to prevent the accumulations that are an injury to business and a temptation to war between nations, but it would tend to secure honesty in making these clearances. Nearly every man is honest when the whole world is looking on.

THE ESSENTIAL CONDITIONS FOR PERMANENT BIMETALLISM.

It is certain that no plan for the use of both silver and gold can possibly be permanently successful, if it provides for the purchase of only a limited amount of silver, nor even for an unlimited amount for a limited time, as was proposed in a plan submitted to the Brussels Conference in 1892. The smallest surplus on the market makes the price of the whole, and there can be no stable money when there are differing coinage and market values for the metal used in it. Even if the amount to be purchased were placed high enough to absorb the total production at the time, the expectation that this would, at a later day, exceed the amount to be taken and that the price would then decline, would bring into the market the hoardings of previous years. If the purchases were large in amount but were ordered for only a limited number of years, everyone, anticipating the "deluge" at the end of that period, would, by forcing sales of accumulated stocks, bring "the deluge" before its expiration.

Neither is it possible to make a plan permanently successful that contemplates the purchase of even unlimited amounts for an unlimited period, if these are to be made on an absolutely unchangeable value-ratio between the metals; for the conditions of production are constantly changing, and at the fixed ratio adopted it might be that the output of one metal, becoming extremely profitable, would be enormous, while the output of the other might be stationary, or even decline because it was unprofitable to produce it at that market price. It is, therefore, absolutely essential for permanent success in any plan for bimetallism, that each metal shall be taken without limit as to quantity or time, and that the value-ratio between the metals shall be flexible and capable of adaptation to varying conditions of production, so as to prevent such an over-production of either as would eventually render the maintenance of the continued circulation of both impossible. These are the essential conditions of permanent bimetallism, and it is certain that they can be secured by this plan.

Since the coins or certificates issued for the metals purchased are redeemable in gold, or if in large amounts, in gold and silver, a change of ratio will not affect the holder of the coin or certificate therefor. A change of ratio would only require that each country deduct from the value of so much of its money as is in the depreciated metal one-half the amount by which the ratio has been changed, and add to the value of its stock of the appreciating metal in corresponding degree. If the holdings of the two were of equal value (and, at the ratio of 20 silver to 1 gold the world's stock of the metals in coin are very nearly equal, though the proportions held by individual countries differ), a change in ratio would make no alteration in the total value of the world's stock of money. Thus a very much greater stability in the value of money can be secured under this system of bimetallism than is possible with a single metal for money.

It is evident that changes in the value-ratio of the metals would be made rarely and to but small extent, for the values of the metals would remain absolutely fixed and stable in the open market at the ruling ratio. This has been abundantly proven in the past.

THE POSSIBILITY OF MAINTAINING THE RATIO ADOPTED.

A study of the records, cited on another page, shows in the clearest manner that there has been from very early times a certain, though not uniform, increase in the value of gold as compared with that of silver; or otherwise, a steady, though irregular, depreciation in the value of silver as compared with gold. In the twenty-eight years from 1493 to 1520 the production of silver averaged by weight 8.1 times that of gold, while it required 10¼ of silver to equal 1 of gold in value. The production of gold grew but very slowly during the 107 years from 1493 to 1600, while that of silver increased about 700%, its output averaging in the twenty years ending 1600 no less than 56.8 times that of gold, though its relative value declined only about 10% or to a ratio of 11.8 to 1 gold. During the next century the output of silver actually declined while that of gold increased. The relative weights averaged, from 1680 to 1700, about 31.8 silver to 1 gold, or nearly the same proportion in which the metals are at present produced, yet while it then required only 15 of silver to equal 1 of gold in value, it required in 1892 no less than 23.73 silver to equal 1 of gold, and at the present time it requires about 30 to 1.

During the one hundred and seventy years from 1700 to 1870 the relative values of gold and silver varied only between the limits of 14¼ and 16¼ to 1 (which represented about the average coining ratios) though the production-ratio fluctuated between the limits of 4 and 50 silver to 1 gold. Thus from 1700 to 1720 the production was, by weight, about 28 silver to 1 gold; one hundred years later, in 1800 to 1810, it averaged 50.3 silver to 1 gold, and fifty years later, or from 1850 to 1860, it averaged only 4½ silver to 1 gold. The production of gold had in the last period of ten years attained about 200,000 kilos a year, a figure it never before or since reached. From this maximum it steadily declined until 1884, when it amounted to about 145,000 kilos, and it has since slowly increased until 1892, when it reached 196,000 kilos.

The production of silver has increased more uniformly and rapidly than gold; in 1670 it was about 335,000 kilos a year and in the year 1892 it amounted to nearly 6,000,000 kilos, being then at the ratio of about 30.2 silver to 1 gold by weight; the production and value ratios, being now (July, 1893) temporarily nearly equal.

From this record (see page 37) it is very evident that during all the past, up at least to 1870, the value-ratio of silver and gold was not governed by their production ratio; or otherwise the value of silver as compared with that of gold was not governed by either the actual or the relative production of the white metal; it was in fact maintained almost stationery for the two hundred years preceding 1870, while its actual production increased four-fold, and its relative production fluctuated between 4 and 50 to 1 of gold.

The reason for this stability in value under such widely varying conditions of production is not difficult to find.

There is nothing mysterious or sacred about gold and silver; they are simply commodities whose market values depend, like those of all other commodities, upon supply and demand. The demand for silver previous to 1871, when nearly all the nations had free coinage of silver, took all that was offered at about its average coinage ratio with gold. Whether the amount produced was actually or relatively great or small it found a market in coinage at the coinage ratio; the demand was not so urgent as to induce "a scramble for silver" when its output was only 4 times as great as that of gold, and its market price never advanced materially above the coinage ratio; yet when it was produced in relatively enormous quantities its price did not decline because of this universal use in coinage. Unquestionably the growing wealth of the world as well as the intrinsic properties of the metal have tended to increase a preference, which seems always to have existed, for the more valuable metal, gold, and to widen its use in money, thus tending to restrict that of silver.

Germany, in December, 1871, assumed the sovereign right of coinage, adopted the gold standard and discontinued the mintage of the silver standard, and in July, 1873, it commenced the sale of its silver and thereby forced France, and in the following year the whole Latin Union, to limit its coinage of silver. In February, 1873, the United States, which had then no silver money in circulation, reduced the legal tender right of silver to payments not exceeding five dollars ; thus practically demonetizing it.   In 1874 the Scandinavian States demonetized silver, and in 1875 and 1876 Holland, Switzerland, Belgium, France, Spain, and Russia suspended the mintage of silver except in special cases, for government account.

These various acts greatly curtailed the demand for silver in coinage, and the German sales, added to an increasing production, so overstocked the market that the price of the metal declined below its coining value, a condition which has continued to the present time, notwithstanding the heavy purchases of silver by the United States Treasury under the Bland Act of February, 1878, and later under the Sherman Act of July, 1890.

Under the recent suspension of free silver coinage in India, the market for the metal is still further lessened, and, with the proposed and inevitable stoppage of purchases by the United States Government, to be followed no doubt by the suspension of free coinage in the remaining silver-basis countries, we are brought face to face with a sudden decline in the value of silver, and an appreciation in that of gold, which threaten great financial distress to the whole world.   In only one way, namely by an international agreement for bimetallism, does it seem possible to prevent these impending disasters.

EFFECTS OF THE SUDDEN DEMONETIZATION OF SILVER.

In order to appreciate the first and most direct loss the general demonetization of silver would occasion, we must get some idea of the price to which silver would probably go if the demand for it as a money metal should be limited to its use in subsidiary coinage.

The subsidiary silver coinage of the United States amounts to about $78,000,-000, or rather less than 5 per cent of our total money.   That of Great Britain is about 14 per cent of the total money ; that of Italy, 5 per cent ; Germany, 11 per cent, etc.   It is probable that in poorer countries the proportions would be greater, but if it averaged even 10 per cent of the world's money, it would be but $1,000,000,000, or say one-quarter of the total stock of silver.

The experience of the United States has fully demonstrated that people greatly prefer paper certificates to silver coins, and if silver were demonetized, paper certificates of $1 and upwards would be based on gold and not on fluctuating silver. There would then be practically no use, as money, for the greater part of the $3,000,000,000, and something like 75,000 tons of silver would be in stock, and would have to find a market along with the annual production, while a comparatively small amount annually would supply the requirements for subsidiary coinage.

The physical properties of silver do not render the metal very much more useful in the arts than nickel, aluminum or copper, and would certainly not create for it any *large* uses at a figure at all approaching its present value.   Silver, however, cannot now be produced in quantity at less than about sixty-five cents per ounce; nor does it exist in nature in that abundance which would ever allow it to compete in price with these other metals.

When once the conviction had become general that silver would no longer be a money metal and that its value would depend on its physical properties alone, and would be regulated, as is that of other metals, by the surplus stock on the market, then the demand for silver in the arts would heavily decline, indeed no one would buy silver to-day at 75 cents per ounce if he believed that within a year it would be worth 40 or 20 cents. The glamour of traditional value in money having disappeared and there being an enormous stock of the metal on hand, its price would probably sink not only far below cost of production but even below its intrinsic value as a metal, but where the market price would stop, whether at 50 cents, at 30, at 20 or at 10 cents per ounce, no one can tell. Aside from its use in money it would find such limited use at even 20 cents. an ounce that the stock on hand would supply the market for very many years, and it is unlikely that, if universally demonetized, the present stock could be marketed promptly at even that price. It is true the whole amount might not be sold at the assumed minimum price, but there would also be a considerable loss on the subsidiary coinage, which would have to be increased in weight, to prevent counterfeiting, when the value of the metal declined so heavily.

The actual loss through the demonetization of silver would not by any means be measured by this sudden destruction of say $2,000,000,000 in the value of the world's stock of silver money. The silver-basis nations would necessarily be obliged to buy gold, and adopt the gold standard, and there would quickly result a general "scramble" for the metal. The inhabitants of India would "run for gold," and would buy it at any price with the silver they have. The United States would, very probably, endeavor to greatly increase its holding of gold,—perhaps it might endeavor to buy and hold from $200,000,000 to $500,000,000, issuing bonds to pay for the same.

What would happen if the United States should enter the market to buy even $100,000,000 of gold; the Indian Government and the native Indians even $200,000,000 ; Mexico, South America, Japan, China, and the rest of the silver world even only $300,000,000 of gold ; or in all say $600,000,000, should no European country join in the "scramble"? What would be the effect of an urgent new demand, in the already bare market, for $600,000,000 of the yellow metal ? Where would it come from and to what price would it go? Who can say it would not bring $30 or $40 an ounce, and who can estimate the effect of such an advance in the purchasing power of the then sole standard of values? Would it not close the workshops of the world and bring commerce to a stand? Can any man conceive the horrors and the barbarisms which would be the outcome of destitution and starvation caused by the general stoppage of the wheels of industry ?

The policy of allowing such a problem to "work itself out" is barbarous; its consequences are far too momentous to allow of such ignorant experimenting.

Great Britain is the great commercial, the great creditor nation. She supplies every country with her manufactures and invests her enormous wealth in the securities, the bonds, stocks, mortgages, real estate, etc., of nearly every country. The amount of her holdings of foreign securities has been estimated by eminent authorities at something like $9,000,000,000, or more than the entire amount of the gold and silver money of the world. It is to her interest, infinitely more than to that of any other nation, that the purchasers of her manufactures, those who keep her factories running, the borrowers to whom she lends her wealth, should be prosperous and have a stable money.

England more than any other nation can facilitate a happy solution of the problem; and she, by simply holding back and doing nothing, can precipitate these dangers and disasters which must inevitably follow the sudden change which is now taking place in the standards of values. With England's assent to some such plan as is here proposed that of the world would probably be assured, so that the responsibility for the consequences of failure to adopt it, or the credit for securing this great step in civilization, will rest upon Great Britain.

The United States, the Latin Union, South America, Mexico, India, nearly all other countries, would unquestionably favor a plan which would prevent a sudden change in the value of silver, and that would promise such an immense improvement in their monetary affairs.

The Clearing House Plan does not extend in any dangerous manner the control which every civilized government now exercises over the making of money; it merely simplifies and brings under international supervision the money now used as the world's measure of values, and this control it proposes shall be carried out on the well-tried, and universally successful, lines followed in every country in banking and commercial clearing houses.

Legislatures, as a rule, are not as well qualified to regulate and control monetary transactions as would be an International Clearing House composed of prudent and experienced financiers who would devote their best abilities to this momentous question. No measure which aimed at giving special benefits to one nation at the expense of the others could find acceptance by the majority of such a body.

It is not merely to the interest of every civilized country that there should be a common standard of value, and that none of the existing money of the world should be suddenly destroyed, but it is clearly essential that this money should be subjected to a control that would effectually prevent such pernicious financial practices as have frequently brought great loss and injury on the industries of nations.

Under this plan all existing money would be retained in use, without possibility of either metal going to a premium as compared with the other. The price in the open market of either could not rise materially above its value in money, and any large over-production of either would be effectually prevented through a flexible ratio which would also permit, without disturbance or sudden loss, the gradual evolution towards the use of a single metal, or of some still better measure of value, if that should ever be found desirable.

It is argued that there is a natural evolution towards the sole use of gold, and that this evolution should be allowed to work itself out without interference. There was also a natural evolution going on in Africa through the operation of which the native races of negroes were being exterminated or carried away into slavery, but civilization called for and secured international agreements for the suppression of the slave trade, and stopped or retarded the operation of the law of the survival of the fittest.

There is a natural evolution in the race towards the practice of justice and a regard for the rights of others, whether of the weak or of the strong.   And this practice naturally induces a respect for our own rights, and augments our own prosperity through the increasing welfare it brings to others.

The problem before us for solution is to take the existing conditions, and, by the exercise of justice and enlightened consideration for the interests of the human race, to regulate such changes in the money of the world as will bring us gradually and without disaster to that better system which increasing intercourse has already rendered desirable, and which will soon become absolutely indispensable to that broader civilization to which the evolution of the race is leading us.

This is no narrow question of the profits of a few silver producers, nor of the interests of a state, nor even of the advantage of a single nation ; it is a question affecting the prosperity, the progress in civilization, of the whole human race. Its wise solution will remove the depression and disasters that now hang over the industrial world ; will effectually prevent their recurrence from this cause, and will bring a period of such widespread prosperity as the world has never witnessed.

So mote it be.

MONETARY AND BANKING SYSTEMS OF EUROPE AND BRITISH INDIA.*

GREAT BRITAIN AND COLONIES.

Monetary System.—Up to 1798, England had the double standard, with the legal ratio of gold to silver of 1–15.21. But as, beginning with 1785, the ratio in France was 1 to 15.5, gold coin began to leave England and silver to take its place. To prevent the substition of silver for gold, the English Parliament, in 1798, prohibited the coinage of the white metal. This measure, which was at first intended to be only provisional, soon became definitive, and practically England has had the gold standard since 1798. It became legally, a gold monometallic country, however, only by virtue of the law of June 22, 1816.

The monetary unit—the (sovereign or) pound sterling—is a gold coin weighing 7.988 grams, fineness 0.916⅔; fine gold contained 7,322 grams or 113.001 grains. (The legal gold coins of Great Britain are the sovereign, half-sovereign, two-sovereign, and five-sovereign pieces.) (Actually,) The gold coins consist of sovereigns and half sovereigns.

The silver coins of Great Britain are the crown, double-florin, half-crown, florin, shilling, sixpence, and threepence pieces.

Silver is legal tender only to the amount of £2. The legal ratio in coinage between gold and silver is 1 to 14.28781.

Individuals have a right, under the law, to deposit gold at the royal mint for coinage and to receive therefor £3 17s. 10½d. per ounce of standard gold, but, as a matter of fact, only the Bank of England sends bars to the mint. By the bank act of 1844 that institution is required to receive all the gold brought to it by the public, and pay therefor immediately, at the rate of £3 17s. 9d. per standard ounce. The difference of 1½d. compensates the bank for the loss of interest between the day it deposits the gold at the mint and the day it receives it again in the form of coin, and leaves it besides a small brokerage for its services. (Individuals are aware that if they carried the gold to the mint themselves their losses in interest and other expenses would exceed 1½d., and prefer to sell it directly to the bank.)

Silver is coined only on account of the Government.

The English colonies, Malta, the Cape of Good Hope, Natal; the Australian Colonies, and New Zealand, have the monetary system of the mother country. In Canada, however, the gold dollar of the United States is the monetary unit and the English sovereign is legal tender there at the rate of $4.866.

The single silver standard obtains in the Straits Settlements and Hongkong, where the Mexican dollar is the monetary unit and local tender.

---

* Compiled for use at the Brussels Monetary Conference, 1892, by Mr. Edward Owen Leech, Directo- of the United States Mint.

Banks of Issue.—The Bank of England, founded in 1694, by Montagu obtained its present charter by the bank act of 1844, generally called the Peel act, which regulated the issue of bank notes and prohibited all banks not then banks of issue, to issue notes. The Bank of England is divided into two separate departments, the issue department and the banking department, each independent of the other. Up to the amount of £14,000,000 notes are issued against the public funds and securities in the keeping of the issue department. When one of the banks of issue, other than the Bank of England, goes out of existence or surrenders its right of issue, two-thirds of the amount of its circulation authorized by the act of 1844 go to the Bank of England and add to the number of notes it is authorized to issue on securities representing its capital. Over and above this issue on securities the notes must be guaranteed by a metallic reserve of coin and bullion.

One-fifth of the reserve may be in silver; but in practice no use is made of this power, and issues are made only against gold. The metallic reserve of the issue department is the one that secures the circulation of notes. It is entirely distinct from the reserve of the banking department. At the present time the bank issues notes against £11,015,100, permanent debt of the state to the bank anterior to 1844, plus £5,184,900 on other securities, *i.e.*, immobilized public funds—a total of £16,200,000. Beyond this amount the bank issues notes only against gold coin and bullion.

Besides the Bank of England there are seventy private banks and thirty-seven joint stock banks, authorized to issue £2,678,109 and £2,015,760 respectively.

In Scotland the issue of bank notes is regulated by the act of Parliament of July 21, 1845, based on the same principles as the charter of the Bank of England contained in the act of 1844. The Scotch banks of which the Bank of Scotland is one, may issue, over and above their coin and bullion, notes to the amount of £2,676,350. Ireland has six banks authorized to issue uncovered notes to the amount of £6,354,494.

Estimated Stock of Money in Great Britain.—Gold, $550,000,000, Silver (subsidiary), $100,000,000; Uncovered notes, $50,000,000, being composed of Bank notes, $200,000,000, less Metallic reserves $150,000,000.

BRITISH INDIA.

Monetary System.—The fundamental monetary law of British India bears date August 17, 1835. The standard of the country is silver (monometallic) and the monetary unit the rupee, of the legal weight of 180 troy grains, fineness 0.916⅔, and containing 165 grains of pure silver. The coinage of silver is unlimited, and the mint charge 2½ per cent; (93½ rupees are manufactured out of 1 kilogram of pure silver.)

The silver coins are the 1-rupee, ½-rupee, ¼-rupee, and ⅛-rupee pieces, all of the fineness of the rupee and proportional to it in weight. Large payments are estimated in lacs of 100,000 rupees and in crores of 100 lacs. The rupee and half rupee are unlimited legal tender, provided the coins have not lost more than 2 per cent in weight and have not suffered deterioration otherwise than by abrasion. The quarter rupee and eighth rupee are legal tender only to the amount of fractions of the rupee.

The gold coins are: The mohur or piece of 15 rupees; the 10-rupee piece, equivalent to two-thirds of a mohur; the 5-rupee piece, equivalent to the one-third of a mohur, and the double mohur or 30-rupee piece. The weight of the mohur is 180 troy grains, 0.916⅔ fine and contains 165 grains of pure gold. The other gold coins are of the same fineness as the mohur and have a weight proportional to it. Gold is not legal tender in India. There is a coinage charge of 1 per cent for gold. The ratio of gold to silver in coinage is 1 to 15.

Banks of Issue.—Previous to the law of July 16, 1861, providing for the issue of a paper currency through a government department of public issue, by means of promissory notes, there were three "chartered banks of India" authorized to issue bank notes to the amount of 52,000,000 rupees, a privilege of which that law deprived them. Geographical circles of issue have since then been established from time to time, the notes made legal tender within the circle for which they were issued, and rendered payable at the place of issue as well as at the capital of the presidency.

At present there are eight circles of issue, which give notes ranging from 5 to 10,000 rupees in value, in exchange for coin.

The amount of currency notes in circulation on the 31st of March, 1892, was 240,764,085 rupees. Upward of 66 per cent of this amount was covered by coin and bullion and the remainder by government securities.

Estimated Stock of Money in British India.—Silver (full tender), $900,-000,000; Currency notes, $100,000,000.

THE LATIN UNION.—FRANCE, BELGIUM, ITALY, SWITZERLAND, AND GREECE.

Monetary System.—Previous to the formation of the Latin Union, there had existed a *de facto* monetary union between France, Belgium, Italy, and Switzerland, the three latter countries having adopted the system established by the French law of (the 17th of Germinal, year XI) April 6, 1803, the basis and monetary unit of which was the silver franc, and which granted legal currency to gold at the ratio in coinage of gold to silver of 1 to 15½.

The change, however, in the commercial ratio of the value of the precious metals, consequent on the enormous production of gold in California and Australia, caused an ever-increasing substitution of gold for silver in the monetary systems of these countries. In the years 1850–1865 silver began to be exported from them, and a great dearth of silver coins to be felt. To remedy these evils, by providing a uniform metallic currency system for these countries, was the chief incentive that led to the Monetary Convention of December 22, 1865, and to the formation of the Latin Union. The contracting states maintained the double standard and the existing ratio of value of 1 to 15½, but limited the standard silver coins to be stamped to the 5-franc silver piece. During the deliberations of the Conference, the delegates of Belgium, Italy, and Switzerland advocated the abolition of that coin and the introduction of the single gold standard, but their endeavors were frustrated by the influence of the French

Government.   All silver coins of less value than the 5-franc piece, *i. e.*, the 2, 1, ½, and ⅕ franc pieces, were transformed into divisional coins.

Thus the system of the Union, under the convention of 1865, became identical with that established for France by the law of April 6, 1803, and its subsequent amendments by the French Parliament.   The law of·April 6, 1803, provided that 5 grains of silver, 0.900 fine, should constitute the monetary unit and be called the franc.   But the basis of the monetary system of that year exists in the system of the.Latin Union only in the 5-franc silver piece, the 1-franc piece having been reduced to a fineness of 0.835.

By the Convention of 1865, each of the contracting states obligated itself to receive into its treasuries the coins manufactured by the others, without limitation as to the value, in the case of gold coins and 5-franc silver pieces, and to the amount of 100 francs in the case of other silver pieces in any one payment.   It was further stipulated that the latter should be legal tender in the country that issued them, to the amount of 50 francs, between private parties in any one payment ; and that they should be taken back by such country and exchanged for gold or 5-franc silver pieces, this obligation to be prolonged during the two years beginning with the expiration of the Convention.   The nominal value of the divisional silver coins, under this convention, being greater than their intrinsic value, because of the lowering of their fineness, their coinage was reserved to the states respectively, and limited to 6 francs per capita of the population of each.   This first convention of the Latin Union, to which Greece became a party in 1867, was concluded for a period of fifteen years, with a provision for tacit renewal.   It maintained the fineness of 0.900 for the 5-franc silver piece, and provided for the free coinage of both metals, thus putting the Latin Union under the bimetallic system.   The depreciation of silver which began in 1872, forced the contracting powers first to limit and then to suspend the coinage of the 5-franc silver piece.

These measures were taken in fulfillment of special Conventions dated January 31, 1874; April 26, 1875; February 3, 1876. and November 5, 1878, and were sanctioned by the Conventions of November 5, 1878, and November 6, 1885.

The Convention of the 23d of December, 1865, expired on the 1st of January, 1880.   A new Convention of the 5th of November, 1878, prolonged the duration of the Latin Union for five years.   The Convention now in force is dated November 6, 1885.   By its terms the suspension of the coinage of the 5-franc silver piece is maintained in the countries of the Union ; but any of the contracting states may resume the free coinage of silver on condition of exchanging during the entire duration of the Convention, the 5-franc silver pieces bearing its stamp and circulating in the other states of the Union, for gold, on demand. The latter, however, would then be at liberty not to receive the 5-franc silver pieces of the state that resumed the free coinage of the white metal.   It was likewise stipulated in the Convention of 1885 that the coins of each of the signatory powers should be received by the treasuries of the others as well as by the banks of France and Belgium, and that the Union might be terminated any time after January 1, 1891, by giving one year's notice.

During the year following the termination of the Convention, the several goverments are to proceed to the exchange and return to the country, that issued them, of the 5-franc silver pieces. Any balance remaining after the exchange has to be settled in gold, or bills of exchange, on the debtor state. Belgium, however, is obliged to pay France only one-half the balance, and Switzerland only 6,000,000 francs, in this way, but has obligated itself not to introduce into its monetary system for five years any change which might hinder the return to it of the other half, by the way of trade, and has guaranteed that this half shall not exceed 200,000,000 francs. In Italy's case, the maximum of the 5-franc pieces it has to take back from Switzerland is fixed at 30,000,000 francs, and the minimum balance from France at the proportion agreed upon between the latter country and Belgium.

In brief, therefore, the Latin Union has the double standard and the ratio of gold to silver of 1 to $15\frac{1}{2}$; (3,100 francs being coined out of the kilogram of tandard gold, and 200 francs out of the kilogram of standard silver; $3,444\frac{4}{9}$ francs out of the kilogram of pure gold, and $222\frac{2}{9}$ francs out of the kilogram of pure silver.) The coinage of gold is unlimited, and that of silver suspended. The coinage charge of $7\frac{4}{9}$ francs per kilogram fine for gold, and $1\frac{3}{5}$ francs per kilogram fine for silver. Gold coins and the 5-franc silver pieces are unlimited legal tender.

Gold Coins.	Legal weight. Grams.	Fineness.	Fine weight Grams.
100 francs	82.258	.900	29, 32
50 francs	16.129	.900	14.516
20 francs	6.452	.900	5.806
10 francs	3.226	.900	2.903
5 francs	1.613	.900	1.452

The franc is known as the lire in Italy, and as the drachma in Greece. The only full legal tender silver coin is the 5-franc piece, legal weight, 25 grams; fineness, 0.900; fine weight, 22.5 grams.

Silver Coins.	Legal weight. Grams.	Fineness.	Fine weight. Grams.
2 francs	10	.835	8.35
1 franc	5	.835	4.18
50 centimes	2.5	.835	2.088
20 centimes	1	.835	0.835

The centime is called the centesimo (plural centesimi) in Italy, and the lepton (plural lepta) in Greece. These silver coins are legal tender between individuals to the amount of 50 francs, and are receivable by the state to the amount of 100 francs in single payments.

*Banks of Issue in the Latin Union.—France.—*The only bank of issue in France is the Bank of France. Its capital belongs entirely to its shareholders and it is in no sense a state bank. The governor and the two subgovernors of the bank, however, are appointed by decree of the President of the Republic. It was founded on the 13th of February, 1800, with a capital of 30,000,000 francs, which was increased to 45,000,000 in 1803, to 90,000,000 in 1806, to 91,250,000 in 1848, and to 182,500,000 francs in 1857. Its charter, granted originally for fifteen years, was renewed several times, the last time on June 9, 1857, for a period of forty years. It will not expire until December 31, 1897. The renewal of its charter is now under discussion in the French Chambers. There is no doubt of its renewal, but on what terms, especially for how long a period, is a question which is being warmly debated. The state has no share in its profits. The direct taxes it is required to pay are 3 per cent. on its dividends, stamp duties on its shares and notes in circulation, and various other stamp duties. Its capital is represented by 182,500 shares of the nominal value of 1,000 francs each.

There is no charter limitation on the amount of notes the bank may issue, but its note circulation has been successively limited by law to 350,000,000 francs, 452,000,000, 525,000,000, 1,800,000,000, 2,400,000,000, 2,800,000,000, and finally, by the law of January 30, 1884, to 3,500,000,000.

The notes of the bank are legal tender at the public treasuries and between private parties, so long as they are redeemed by the bank on demand. The issue of notes within the limit fixed by law and the proportion to be observed betweed the amount of circulation and the metallic reserve are left to the discretion of the government of the bank.

Belgium.—The National bank of Belgium, established by the law of May 5, 1850, is the only joint stock company authorized in Belgium to issue notes payable to the bearer at sight; but individuals and associations are free to issue bank notes on their own responsibility. The National Bank of Belgium is not, properly speaking, a state bank, although the treasury receives a large share of its profits fixed at first at one-sixth and since 1872 at one-fourth of the profits it realizes over and above 6 per cent. It also receives one-fourth per cent. on the average circulation of the bank over 275,000,000 francs. Receipts from discounts go to the state if the rate exceeds 5 per cent. The Government does not interfere in the management of the bank, but may veto any measure which it deems opposed to the bank's charter, the law, or the interest of the state.

The bank, located in Brussels, has a branch at Anvers and agencies throughout the Kingdom. Its capital is 50,000,000 francs, divided into 50,000 shares, (of the nominal value of 1,000 francs each.) The issue of notes is not limited in an absolute manner, but the law requires that it should be represented by securities which may be easily realized upon, and that the bank should have a metallic reserve (unless otherwise authorized in special cases by the minister of finance) equal to one-third of the obligations it must meet on demand. The notes of the bank have legal but not forced currency, and are in denominations of 1,000 500, 100, 50, and 20 francs. It is the financial agent of the treasury.

Italian Banks.—Italy has no state bank. There are in the country six banks of issue, which, by virtue of the law of April 30, 1874, are authorized to issue notes payable on demand, to the amount, as an extreme limit, of three times their paid-up capital. But the total of the notes and obligations immediately payable, arising from deposits and accounts current, at sight, must not exceed three times the amount of coin and bullion in the banks. Their notes have not legal currency. All issue notes are of 50, 100, 500, and 1,000 lire. By the law of 1874 on forced currency, the six banks were authorized to issue a maximum circulation as follows, but have not always kept within the legal limit:

National Bank of the Kingdom, 450,000,000 francs; Roman Bank, 45,000,000 francs; National Bank of Tuscany, 63,000,000 francs; Tuscan Bank of Credit, 15,000,000 francs; Bank of Naples, 146,250,000 francs; Bank of Sicily, 36,-000,000 francs. Total, 755,250,000 francs.

Since the abolition of forced currency, this limit has been done away with in the interest of the monetary circulation, and the banks of issue have been authorized to emit additional notes provided the excess is covered by a second metallic reserve (of two-thirds gold and one-third silver) to an equal amount.

These six institutions formed, in 1874, a syndicate to lend the Government a sum of 1,000,000,000 lire, and to issue notes in representation thereof, of the denominations of 1,000, 250, 100, 20 and 10 francs. When forced currency was abolished in 1874, the syndicate was dissolved and the syndicate notes became a state debt.

Swiss Banks.—The banks of issue in Switzerland, some founded by individual enterprise and others with Cantonal assistance, are of comparatively recent institution. The oldest is that of St. Gall, established in 1836. The Swiss federal law on the issue and redemption of bank notes is dated March 8, 1881.

Previous governmental authorization is necessary to the establishment of a bank of issue. The number of such banks is not limited. The Federal Assembly reserves the right of fixing at all times the total issue of the Republic, and determining the quota of each bank. The banks are required to hold a metallic reserve, distinct and independent of all other reserves of the bank, equal at least to 40 per cent. of their circulation, while the remaining 60 per cent must be covered by securities readily convertible. The Government has no power to create a monopoly bank of issue, nor to endow the notes of the several banks with forced currency; but each bank is required to take the notes of the other banks in payment, and to procure the redemption of the notes of other banks without compensation.

Banks of Greece.—Greece has three banks authorized to issue notes, but these have forced currency ; the metallic reserves are merely nominal, and the country at this time is so completely under an irredeemable paper money régime that it may be said to have no bank-of-issue system.

Estimated Stock of Money in the Latin Union.—Gold, $975,000,000 ; Silver (full legal) $727,000,000 ; Silver (limited tender,) 95,000,000 ; Uncovered notes $250,000,000 ; being Bank notes, $925,000,000 less Metallic reserve, $675,-000,000.

SPAIN.

Monetary System.—By a decree of the 19th of October, 1868, Spain adopted the monetary system of the Latin Union. It is therefore, bimetallic with the silver peseta, equivalent to the franc, as monetary unit. It has the same gold and silver coins as the Union. A gold 25-peseta piece was added by a decree of August 20, 1876.

SILVER COINS.	Legal weight. Grams.	Fineness.	Fine weight. Grams.
5 pesetas	25	.900	22.5
2 pesetas	10	.835	8.35
1 peseta	5	.835	4.175
Half peseta	2.5	.835	2.0875
Fifth peseta	1	.835	0.835

GOLD COINS.	Legal weight. Grams.	Fineness.	Fine weight. Grams.
100 pesetas	32.25808	.900	29.0323
50 pesetas	16.12903	.900	14.5161
25 pesetas	8.06451	.900	7.2581
20 pesetas	6.4516	.900	5.8064
10 pesetas	3.2258	.900	2.9032
5 pesetas	1.6129	.900	1.4516

The coinage of gold is free, and there is no coinage charge for that metal, but depositors cannot get the coined gold until eighteen days after the delivery of the bullion to the mint. Since 1878 silver has been coined only on account of the state. The ratio of gold to silver is 1 to 15½ gold and the 5-peseta silver piece are unlimited legal tender ; divisional silver coin, *i. e.*, all silver coins of less value than 5 francs, only to the amount of 50 pesetas.

Banks of Issue.—The only bank of issue in the country is the Bank of Spain, founded in 1829, reorganized in 1856, with a franchise of twenty-five years, which was renewed in 1874 for a period of thirty years. It has enjoyed the exclusive privilege of issuing bank notes, however, only since March 19, 1874. The law of that date raised its capital to 100,000,000 pesetas, divided into 200,000 shares (of the nominal value of 500 pesetas.) Since then it has been raised to 150,000,000. The eighteen provincial banks of issue existing at that time have been liquidated. The bank is not a state bank, and the state has no share in its profits. The state, however, may require of it advances, on sufficient security, to the maximum amount of 125,000,000 pesetas. It is located at Madrid, with branches in the principal cities. It has a reserve fund equal to 10 per cent. of its paid-up capital. Any diminution of this reserve fund has to be made good from the yearly profits over and above 6 per cent. It is authorized to issue bank notes to an amount equal to five times its paid-up capital, or 750,000,000 pesetas ; but may not, under any circumstances, issue more than four times its metallic reserve. Its notes have legal currency, and are of denominations of 1,000, 500, 100, 50, and 25 pesetas.

Estimated Stock of Money.—Gold $40,000,000 ; Silver, (full tender,) 120,000,-000 ; Silver, (limited tender,) $38,000,000 ; Uncovered notes, $100,000,000 ; being Bank notes, $165,000,000, less Metallic reserve, $65,000,000.

THE NETHERLANDS.

Monetary System.—When England in 1816 adopted the gold standard, the Netherlands, which then had the single silver standard, went over to the double standard, with the ratio of gold to silver of 1 to 15.873. They returned in 1847 to the silver standard, and afterwards, in 1875, again replaced the latter by the double standard. The fundamental monetary laws of the coutry at the present time are those of November 26, 1847, and June 6, 1875. The monetary unit is the guilder or florin, of 100 cents.

The standard gold coins are the 10-florin and 5-florin pieces. The 10-florin piece has a legal weight of 6.720 grams, 0.900 fine, and contains 6.048 grams of fine gold. The 5-florin piece is not coined at present.

Silver Coins.	Legal weight. Grams,	Fineness.	Fine weight, Grams.
Florin...	10	.945	9 450
Half florin	5	.945	4.725
Rixdaler 2½ florin)....................................	25	.945	23.625
25-cent piece..	3.575	.640	2.288
10-cent piece..	1.400	.640	0.896
5-cent piece...	0.685	.640	0.438

The trade coins are the double ducat and the ducat, 0.983 fine, and containing respectively, 6.8692 and 3.4346 grams of pure metal.

(Out of a kilogram of pure gold there are manufactured 1,653.43 florins, and out of a kilogram of pure silver 105.82 florins.)

Only the standard gold and silver coins are unlimited legal tender. Silver fractional coins are legal tender to the amount of 10 florins.

The coinage of gold is free; that of standard silver coins, except on account of the state, has been suspended since December 9, 1877.

The coinage of fractional silver is on Government account. The coinage charges are 5 florins per kilogram of gold and 1 florin per kilogram of silver.

The monetary system of the Netherland colonies is the same as that of the mother country.

Banks of Issue.—The Bank of the Netherlands, founded in 1814, has the exclusive right to issue notes. Its charter has been renewed three times, each times for twenty-five years. It last expired March 31, 1889, but was again renewed, and will not now terminate till 1914. The Bank of the Netherlands is not a state bank, but a certain amount of surveillance is exercised over it by a special commissioner of the Kingdom, who is paid by the bank; and its president and secretary are appointed by the King. It is situated at Amsterdam, but has a branch at Rotterdam, and agencies and correspondents in nearly six places in the country. Its capital is 16,000,000 florins. It receives no interest-bearing deposits and its accounts current are payable at sight.

The amount of issue of its notes is not absolutely fixed, but by royal decree the sum total of its notes, of its checks, and balances of account current must be covered to the extent of at least 40 per cent by its metallic reserve, which may consist of gold and silver coin or bullion. Since 1872 the bank has purchased no silver for its reserve. Under the law its only possible debts are its notes, its own checks, and its accounts current.

In addition to the bank notes there are Government notes in circulation to the extent of 15,000,000 florins.

Estimated Stock of Money in the Netherlands.—Gold, $25,000,000; Silver, (full tender), $61,800,000; Silver (limited tender), $3,200,000; Uncovered notes, $40,000,000; being State notes, $8,000,000, plus Bank notes, $82,000,000; less Metallic reserve, $50,000,000.

GERMAN EMPIRE.

Monetary System.—The fundamental laws of the present monetary system of Germany are those of December 4, 1871, and July 9, 1873. The standard is gold (monometallic,) and the monetary unit the mark of 100 pfennige (2,790 gold marks are manufactured from 1 kilogram of fine gold.)

Gold Coins.	Legal weight. Grams.	Fineness.	Fine weight. Grams.
20 marks	7.96495	.900	7.168458
10 marks	3.98247	.900	8.584220
5 marks	1.99123	.900	1.792114

and hence the mark, or monetary unit, contains 0.358422939 gram of pure gold.

The maximum coinage charge for individuals is 14 marks, in the case of 20 mark pieces, per kilogram of fine gold.

The law of the 4th of December, 1871, was concerned exclusively with the creation of the gold coins of the Empire, and provided for the retirement of the old gold coins. It dealt with silver only to authorize the retirement of the current coins of that metal. The law of July 9, 1873, was supplemental to it, and organized the new monetary system.

As to gold, it made no change in the law of 1871, save to authorize the coinage of the 5 mark gold piece, and to allow the coinage of 20-mark gold pieces on private account when the mints were not occupied on account of the state.

The silver coins of the new system, 0.900 fine, are 5-mark, 2-mark, 1-mark, 50 and 20 pfennig pieces, 5 grams of fine silver to a mark. The coinage of silver is solely on account of the state. The total coinage of silver was limited to 10 marks per capita of the population of the Empire. Silver is legal tender to the amount of 20 marks. All these coins are exchangeable for gold at the public treasuries.

In effecting its monetary reform Germany called in all its old silver coins, with the exception of its thalers, which are still in circulation to the amount of about 450,000,000 marks, the thaler being reckoned as equivalent to 3 marks of the new system.

Banks of Issue.—The principal bank of issue in the Empire is the Imperial Bank of Germany, established by the law of March 14, 1875. It succeeded the Bank of Prussia, which was founded in 1765 and reorganized in 1846.

It is not a state bank, its capital having been furnished by its shareholders, but on the expiration of its franchise, and ten years after any renewal of it, the state may, by giving one year's notice in advance of its intention, assume the exercise of the bank's franchise on its own account, either by liquidating it and acquiring its real property at the price at which it figures on the books of the bank, or by purchasing shares at their nominal value. In either case one half of the reserve fund of the bank goes to the shareholders and the other half to the state. The capital of the bank is 120,000,000 marks, divided into 40,000 shares (of the nominal value of 3,000 marks each). Although not a state bank it is intimately connected with the state. The superintendence and direction of it belongs to the chancellor of the Empire, who acts through a council of curators of which he is the president, and which is composed of four members, one appointed by the Emperor and three by the Federal Council. The personnel of the bank are assimilated to the functionaries of the Empire.

Employees are not allowed to hold any shares of the bank. The state shares in the profits of the bank to the average amount of about 2,000,000 marks a year. In 1875, when the bank law was promulgated, there were, Including the Imperal Bank, thirty-three banks of issue in Germany.

Some fifteen of those have surrendered their right to issue bank notes, or have lost their franchise by its expiration.

The uncovered circulation of the Imperial Bank of Germany has no absolute limit, and the amount of such circulation in excess of 296,000,000 marks is subject to a tax of 5 per cent, while the total circulation may not exceed three times the metallic reserve.

Originally, *i. e.* in 1873, the amount of uncovered notes not taxable was fixed at 385,000,000 marks, 250,000,000 of which might be issued by the Imperial Bank, and 135,000,000 by the thirty-two other banks then in existence. The law, however, provided that when any of these latter surrendered or lost its right of emission, the amount of its untaxable notes should be added to those of the Imperial Bank. In this way the amount of the untaxable notes of the Imperial Bank has grown recently to 296,000,000 marks.

The charter of the bank was to have expired on the 1st of January, 1891, but was renewed for ten years in December, 1889. In addition to the bank notes there is a permanent circulation of 120,000,000 marks of treasury notes.

Estimated Stock of Money in the German Empire.—Gold, $600,000,000; Silver (thalers), $103,000,000; Silver (limited tender), $108,000,000; Uncovered Notes, $107,000,000, being, Treasury notes, $28,500,000; plus Bank notes, $315,000,000; less Metallic reserve, $236,500,000.

AUSTRIA-HUNGARY.

Monetary System until the Recent Currency Reform.—The monetary system established in Austria-Hungary by the Imperial patents of September 19, 1857, April 27, 1858; the laws of December 24, 1867, March 9, 1870, and May 21, 1887, was the silver monometallic with the florin of 100 kreutzers as the monetary unit. The silver coins were:

The 2-florin piece, 0.900 fine, containing 22.222 grams of fine silver; the 1-florin piece, 0,900 fine, containing 11.111 grams of fine silver, the quarter-florin piece, 0.520 fine, containing 2.778 grams of fine silver.

The silver divisional coins of Austria-Hungary were: the 20-kreutzer piece, 0.500 fine, containing 1.333 grams fine; the 10-kreutzer piece, 0.400 fine; containing 0.6664 grams fine; these pieces were legal tender among private persons to the amount of 2 florins.

The silver trade coins were the Maria-Theresa or Levantine thalers, fineness 0.833⅓, containing 23.3890 grams of pure silver.

The gold trade coins were the quadruple ducat and ducat, the latter weighing 3.4909 grams, 0.986⅔ fine, and containing 3.4424 grams of pure gold; also the 8-florin and 4-florin pieces equal, in value to the French 20-franc and 5-franc pieces respectively.

The gold ducats were not legal tender. The coinage charges were : One-half per cent for the ducats, 8-florin and 4-florin pieces; 1 per cent for the 2-florin and 1-florin pieces; 2⅓ per cent for the quarter-florin pieces; 1½ per cent for the Maria-Theresa thalers.

The coinage of silver on private account was suspended in January, 1879.

But while Austria-Hungary has been legally a country with a single silver standard, practically it has had no metallic money in circulation. For nearly half a century it has, with the exception of about eight months, had nothing but an irredeemable paper currency issued by the Austro-Hungarian Bank in denominations of 10, 100, and 1,000 florins, and by the treasury of 1, 5, and 50 florins. For a long series of years there was a premium on silver, but since the end of 1878 silver and paper have been at par. The value of the silver florin, owing to the limitation of the coinage of silver, is considerably greater than that of the pure metal it contains.

The Recent Monetary Reform of Austria-Hungary.—The provisions of the recent Austro-Hungarian currency reform are embodied in six bills, the two most important of which are those on the new currency system and on the monetary treaty of Austria with Hungary. These have already become laws. The other four are merely auxiliary to those two which contain the text of the new fundamental monetary law of the two countries. The four auxiliary bills are intended to fix the relative value of the gold florin to the new gold coins; to determine the changes which have become necessary in the bank act; to authorize the Government to raise a gold loan, and to provide for the conversion of certain 5 per cent bonds of free tax.

The new monetary system is gold monometallic, and the gold crown of 100 hellers (farthings) the monetary unit. The new currency is to consist of gold, silver, nickel, and bronze coins. The gold coins provided for are:

(1). The 20-crown piece, weighing 6.775 67 grams of gold, 0.900 fine, or a fine weight of 6. 9756 grams.

(2). The 10-crown piece, weighing 3.3875338 grams of gold, 0.900 fine, or a fine weight of 3.04878 grams.

(3). Besides the gold coins above mentioned there are to be coined as heretofore, and as trade coins, Austrian gold ducats. The 4 and 8 gulden gold pieces are to be no longer coined.

The coinage charge is 4 crowns for 1 kilogram of standard gold for the bank and 6 on individual account.

The new silver coins are :

(1) The 1-crown piece, weighing 5 grams of silver, 0.835 fine, and containing 4.175 grams of pure metal.

(2) The 50-heller piece, weighing 2.5 grams of silver 0.835 fine, and containing 2.0875 grams of pure metal.

The ratio of gold to silver in the new system is 1 to 13.69. Silver is coined only on account of the state.

Silver coins are unlimited legal tender at their nominal value to the state; to private parties to the amount of 50 crowns.

The Levantine or Maria-Theresa silver thalers continue to be stamped as trade coins with the old-weight and fineness.

The monetary agreement between Austria and Hungary provides that there shall be coined in all by the two countries 200,000,000 crowns in silver coins, of which Austria's share is 140,000,000 crowns.

The agreement is to remain in force until the end of 1910. Arrangements are to be made at a proper time for the regulation of the fiduciary circulation and the resumption of specie payments.

Austrian paper-money is to remain in circulation provisionally. The paper florin is, like the silver florin, to be worth 2 crowns.

The introduction of the coins of the new system will be made by degrees, in the course of several years, during which time the coins of the old silver standard as well as the state notes will remain current, the coins of the new ssytem multiplied by two, are to be of the same value as the pieces of the old silver and paper currency, 1 silver or paper florin, for instance, being equal to 2 crowns and 1 kreutzer to 2 heller. The value of the new crown is $0.2026 against $0.482, the value of the gold florin.

Banks of Issue in Austria-Hungary.—The Austro-Hungarian Empire has only one bank of issue, the Bank of Austria-Hungary. It does not belong to the state, nor does the Government have any direct share in its administration. The state has no part in the annual profits of the bank, but has received from it a credit of 80,000,000 florins for which it is required to pay an annual sum of only 1,000,000 at most, provided that amount is necessary to make up a dividend of 7 per cent or cause the dividend of the bank to approximate to that maximum rate. The bank, however, pays several taxes, aggregating from 12 to 13 per cent of its profits of late years.

The issue of notes over and above 200,000,000 florins, must be covered by a corresponding amount in legal coin or in bullion. Moreover, the amount of notes of a value exceeding that of the metallic reserve must be guaranteed by discounted paper or by other safe security as well as by the bank itself.

The permanent debt of the state to the bank is 80,000,000 florins.

Its charter, which expired in 1888, was renewed for ten years. In addition to the bank notes there are state notes to the amount of nearly 400,000,000 florins.

Estimated Stock of Money in Austria-Hungary.—Gold, $40,000,000 ; Silver, (full legal) $90,000,000 ; Uncovered notes, $260,000,000 ; being Government notes, $200,000,000; plus Bank notes, 200,000,000, less Metallic reserve, $140,000,000.

SCANDINAVIAN UNION.

Monetary System.—The Scandinavian Monetary Union embraces Sweden, Norway and Denmark. These three kingdoms concluded in 1873 and 1875 a monetary convention based on the employment of the single gold standard and on a common system of coins and money of account. The krone or crown, divided into 100 öre, is the monetary unit.

GOLD.	Legal weight. Grams.	Fineness.	Fine weight. Grams.
20 kronen	8.9606	.900	8.06452
10 kronen	4.4803	.900	4.03226
SILVER.			
2 kronen	15.000	.800	12.000
1 krone	7.500	.800	6.000
50 öre	5.000	.600	3.000
40 öre	4.000	.600	2.400
25 öre	2.420	.600	1.452
10 öre	1.450	.400	0.580

(2,480 kronen are manufactured out of 1 kilogram of fine gold.) The coinage of gold is unlimited. The coinage charges for gold are one-quarter per cent per kilogram fine for 20-kronen pieces, and one-third per cent per kilogram fine for 10 kronen pieces. Silver is coined only on account of the Government.

Silver coins are legal tender as follows :

The 2-kronen and 1-krone pieces to the amount of 20 kronen ; the 50, 40, 25, and 10 öre pieces to the amount of 5 kronen.

All the coins above mentioned have legal currency in the three Kingdoms. The Monetary Convention does not limit the coinage by the governments of the silver or bronze coins. In each of the three states there are public treasuries at which any sum of fractional coin divisible by 10 kronen may be exchanged for gold.

Banks of Issue in the Countries of the Scandinavian Union.—Sweden.—Sweden has a state bank of issue, called the Bank of Sweden, whose capital belongs to the nation ; whose profits may figure in the budget ; and whose administration is confided to a commission elected annually by the Diet.

Banks of issue may be established by joint stock companies with the authorization of the King. Their charters run for ten years and may be renewed. The responsibility of the shareholders is unlimited. There are some thirty of these banks, and the right to issue notes belongs to them jointly with the Bank of Sweden. The latter's capital is fixed at 25,000,000 crowns and its reserve fund at 5,000,000. The constitution guarantees the legal currency of its notes. Its circulation is limited by the law to a fixed sum of 30,000,000 crowns plus, the amount of its credits and accounts current with foreign banks and its metallic reserve, which must not fall below 10,000,000 crowns. The notes of the private banks have only fiduciary currency, and are redeemable in gold only, and not in the notes of the Bank of Sweden. Only the notes of the bank of the state are receivable at the public treasuries. The circulation of a private bank may not exceed the total of the following sums:

The amount of the company's capital converted into mortgages; the part of its reserve invested in mortgage titles; one-half the total credits of the bank; the whole of its metallic stock less a reserve in gold equivalent to 10 per cent of the company's capital. The Bank of Sweden issues about four-ninths and the private banks, about five-ninths of the total notes in circulation in the Kingdom.

Norway.—Norway has only one central bank of issue—the Bank of Norway, founded in 1814. It is a joint stock bank with the state as principal shareholder, and is under the direction of state officials. Its capital is 10,000,000 kronen. Its issue of notes, which have legal currency in the country, may not exceed twice its metallic reserve, but the bank is authorized to place one-third of that reserve with its correspondents in foreign countries.

Denmark.—The National Bank of Denmark, founded in 1818, is the only bank of issue in the Kingdom. Its capital is 27,000,000 kronen, and its issue of notes may, by royal decree of 1877, exceed its Metallic reserve by 30,000,000 kronen.

Estimated Stock of Money in Scandinavian Union.—Gold, $32,000,000; Silver (subsidiary), $10,000,000; Uncovered notes, $27,000,000; being Bank notes, $60,000,000; less Metallic reserve, $33,000,000.

PORTUGAL.

Monetary System.—The present monetary system of Portugal was established by the law of July 29, 1854, and is gold monometallic with the milreis of 1,000 reis as monetary unit. One thousand milreis, or a million reis, is called a conto.

GOLD COINS.	Legal weight. Grams.		Fineness.		Fine weight. Grams.
Crown or 10 milreis.............................	17.735	....	.916¾	....	16.2569
Half crown or 5 milreis..........................	8.868	....	.916⅔	....	8.1284
Fifth crown or 2 milreis	3.547	....	.916⅔	....	3.2513
Tenth crown or 1 milreis.........................	1.774	....	.916⅔	....	0.6256
SILVER COINS.	Legal weight. Grams.		Fineness.		Fine weight. Grams.
5 testones or 500 reis............................	12.5	....	.915¾	....	11.4582
2 tes ones or 200 reis...........................	5.0	....	.916⅔	....	4.5833
Testone or 100 reis..............................	2.5	....	.916⅔	..	2.2916
Half testone or 50 reis..........	1.25	....	.916⅔	....	1.1458

Gold is coined in unlimited amounts on private account at a mint charge of 1 milreis per kilogram.

Silver, like copper, is coined only in divisional coins.

Silver is legal tender only to the amount of 5 milreis, but by Lisbon commercial usage one-third of all payments are accepted in that metal.

Banks of Issue.—The Bank of Portugal, founded in 1822, and seven others. are authorized to issue notes. The notes of the Bank of Portugal are received by the public treasuries but otherwise have not legal currency.

The notes of the other banks are not received by the public treasuries but have currency in their respective districts. By the law of 1854 bank notes should represent gold exclusively and be paid in that metal.

Estimated Stock of Money in Portugal.—Gold, $40,000,000; Silver (limited tender), $10,000,000; Uncovered notes, $45,000,000; being Bank notes, $50,000,-000; less Metallic reserve, $5,000,000.

RUSSIA.

Monetary System.—The fundamental monetary law of the country is dated December 17, 1885. and went into force January 1, 1886. The monetary unit is the silver ruble of . 100 kopecks. The law provides for the coinage of both gold and silver in the ratio of 1 to 15½; the system is, therefore, bimetallic. The gold coins are the imperial (10 rubles) and half-imperial (5 rubles,) of the legal weight of 12.9039 and 6.4519 grams, respectively, and the fineness of 0.900. The imperial therefore contains 11.6135 grams of pure gold and the half-imperial 5.8067. The coinage of gold on private account is unlimited, and the mint charge is 3 per cent for that metal.

The full legal tender silver coins are the ruble, ½-ruble, and ¼-ruble pieces. The silver ruble has a legal weight of 19.995 grams, a fineness of 0.900, and contains 17.996 grams of fine silver.

The half and quarter rubles are of the same fineness and of proportional weight. The divisional coins of Russia are of silver and copper.

Silver Divisional Coins.	Legal weight. Grams.		Fineness.		Fine weight. Grams.
20 kopecks	3.599	....	.500	....	1.799
15 kopecks	2.699	....	.500	....	1.349
10 kopecks	1.799	....	.500	....	0.899
5 kopecks	0.899	....	.500	....	0.499

These coins are legal tender to the amount of 3 rubles between individuals and unlimited legal tender to the state for taxes, etc.

The coinage of silver on private account is suspended.

Such is the monetary system of Russia as it stands upon the statute book, but it has no existence in fact, that country having been under an exclusively paper régime since 1855.

Banks of issue.—The National Bank of Russia is the only bank of issue in the Empire. It is a state bank, established by an imperial ukase in 1860. whose capital and reserve fund were furnished by the Government. Its present capital is 25,000,000 rubles, and its reserve fund 3,000,000. These are the inviolable property of the bank, which the state cannot touch nor use for the public expense any more than it can the deposits of the bank. The state shares the profits of the bank, inasmuch as they are employed as a sinking fund to redeem the notes of the bank, at 5 per cent interest, and to pay other loans made by the state of the bank. It is under the jurisdiction of the minister of finance. Its governor and vice-governor are appointed by the Emperor, and its directors are chosen by the minister of finance on the recommendation of the governor. The bills of credit, or paper money, of Russia are issued by the bank, and hence are not, properly speaking, paper money of the Government.

These credit rubles, in denominations of 1, 3, 5, 10, 25, and 100 rubles, have legal and, as a matter of fact, forced currency since the cessation of specie payments. The amount of credit notes it may issue would seem to depend entirely on the exigencies of the Government.

Estimated Stock of Money in Russia.—Gold, $250,000,000 ; silver, (full tender) $22,000,000 ; silver, (limited tender) $38,000,000 ; Uncovered notes, $500,000,000 ; being Bank notes, $800,000,000, less Metallic reserve, $300,000,-000.

TURKEY.

Monetary System.—The monetary system of Turkey is bimetallic, with the piaster, equal to 40 paras, 3 aspes, as monetary unit. The gold coins are the 500. 250, 100, 50, and 25 piaster pieces, all of the same fineness, viz.: 0.916 ⅔. The 1 -piaster piece, or gold medjidie, is called the Turkish pound. It has a gross weight of 7.216 grams and a fine weight of 6.6146 grams. The gross and fine weight of the other gold coins are proportional to those of the Turkish pound. The silver coins are the 20, 10, 5, 2, 1, and a half piaster pieces 0.830 fine. The 20 piaster piece has a gross weight of 24.055 grams, and a fine weight of 19.9656 grams. The 10, 5. 2, 1, and half-piasters have a proportional gross and fine weight. The ratio of gold to silver was originally 1 to 15.09. By a decree the Government lowered the value of the 20-piaster piece to 19 piasters, in consequence of which debasement the ratio of gold to silver is 1 to 15¾.

The coinage of silver is suspended. The mint charge for gold is 1 per cent. Such is the system as it exists on paper, but the actual coined money of the country is in a very unsatisfactory condition.

Bank of Issue.—The only bank of issue in Turkey is the Imperial Ottoman Bank. Its notes are payble exclusively in gold. Its reserve is generally greater than its circulation. Thus, at the end of 1886 it had a circulation of $1,758,-500, and a reserve of $6,150,000. At present it has a reserve of about $6,285,-000, and a note circulation of only $3,513,000.

ROUMANIA.

Monetary System.—The laws of April 14, 1867, and April 3 , 1879, introduced the system of the Latin Union into Roumania, the franc being called the lei, and the centime the bani ; but in 1890, a measure was passed by the Roumanian Chamber, abrogating the double standard, and substituting for it the single gold standard with a subsidiary silver coinage having a paying power to the amount of 50 lei or francs.

Bank of Issue.—The only bank of issue is the National Bank of Roumania. The law of 1890 introducing the single standard into the country limited the issue of its notes in the proportion of 2½ paper to 1 of gold.

On the 8th of August, 1892, its metallic reserve was 52,400,000 lei, and its circulation 113,342,000 lei.

There are government notes outstanding to the amount of about 125,000,000 lei.

SERVIA.

Monetary System.—The monetary system of Servia was assimilated to that of the Latin Union by the law of November 11, 1878. The franc is called the dinar, and the centime the para. It was provided that after the gold pieces had been put in circulation the 5-dinar pieces should be legal tender only to the amount of 500 dinars, and the smaller silver pieces only to the amount of 50 dinars, thus making the country, practically, gold monometallic.

Bank of Issue.—The only bank of issue of the country is the National Bank of Servia, located at Belgrade, with a branch at Nisch. Its issue may not exceed three times its metallic reserve. Its circulation, on the 3 th of June. 1892, was 25,400,000 dinars, and its metallic reserve 11,000,000 dinars.

The following statistical tables are taken from "The Mineral Industry, its Statistics, Technology and Trade in the United States and Other Countries, From the Earliest Times to end of 1892, being the Statistical Supplement of the *Engineering and Mining Journal.*"

This great volume contains, besides these extracts, a vast amount of other statistical data relating to the production, markets and uses of gold and silver, and of all other metals throughout the world. It is published and copyrighted by the Scientific Publishing Co., New York.

The World's Production of Gold and Silver.

In order to appreciate the gold and silver production of the United States it is necessary to make comparison with that of the world, and to do this intelligently it is imperative to investigate the differing statistics of the world's production, and to reduce from all the data available the most probable figures. The following table is taken from Dr. Adolph Soetbeer's *Materials toward the Elucidation of the Economic Conditions affecting the Precious Metals,* and completed to 1892 from other reliable data:

WORLD'S PRODUCTION OF GOLD AND SILVER.

Period.	Mean Annual Product, Kilos.		Ratio of Silver to Gold, Weight.	Ratio of Gold to Silver, Value.	Period.	Mean Annual Product, Kilos.		Ratio of Silver to Gold, Weight.	Ratio of Gold to Silver, Value.
	Gold.	Silver.				Gold.	Silver.		
1493-1520...	5,800	47,000	8.1	(a)10.75	1856-1860..	201,750	904,990	4.5	15.29
1521-1544...	7,160	90,200	12.6	(b)11.25	1861-1865..	185,057	1,101,150	5.9	15.41
1545-1560...	8,510	311,600	36.6	(c)11.30	1866-1870..	195,026	1,339,085	6.9	15.56
1561-1580...	6,840	299,500	43.8	11.50	1871-1875..	173,904	1,969,425	11.3	15.98
1581-1600...	7,380	418,900	56.8	11.80	1876....	166,956	2,323,779	14.0	17.88
1601-1620...	8,520	422,900	49.6	12.25	1877....	179,445	2,388,612	13.3	17.22
1621-1640...	8,300	393,600	47.4	14.00	1878....	185,847	2,551,364	13.7	17.94
1641-1660...	8,770	366,300	41.8	14.50	1879....	167,307	2,507,507	15.0	18.40
1661-1680...	9,260	337,000	36.4	15.00	1880....	163,515	2,479,998	15.2	18.05
1681-1700...	10,765	341,900	31.8	14.97	1881....	158,864	2,592,639	16.3	18.16
1701-1720...	12,820	355,600	27.7	15.21	1882....	148,475	2,789,065	18.6	18.19
1721-1740...	19,080	431,200	22.6	15.08	1883....	144,727	2,746,123	19.0	18.64
1741-1760...	24,610	533,145	21.7	14.75	1884....	153,193	2,788,727	18.2	18.57
1761-1780...	20,705	652,740	31.5	14.79	1885....	159,289	2,993,805	18.6	19.41
1781-1800...	17,790	879,060	49.4	15.09	1886....	159,741	2,902,471	18.2	20.78
1801-1810...	17,778	894,150	50.3	15.61	1887....	159,155	2,990,398	18.8	21.13
1811-1820...	11,445	540,770	47.2	15.51	1888....	159,809	3,385,606	21.2	21.99
1821-1830...	14,216	460,560	32.4	15.80	1889....	185,809	3,901,609	21.0	22.09
1831-1840...	20,289	596,450	29.4	15.75	1890....	181,256	4,180,532	23.1	19 76
1841-1850...	54,759	780,415	14.3	15.83	1891....	189,824	4,479,649	23.6	20.92
1851-1855...	199,388	886,115	4.4	15.41	1892....	196,234	5,935,315	30.2	23.73

(a) For the period 1501-20; (b) 1521-40; (c) 1541-60.

NOTE.—The figures from 1493-1882, both years inclusive, are Soetbeer's; those for 1882-92 are from the reports of the Director of the Mint, except United States silver for 1892, which is from direct returns of U. S. refiners, etc.

The world's stock of gold and silver was exceedingly small when America was discovered, 1492. Chevalier estimates the stock in Europe at that time at only $193,000,000. It was greater in Asia, where some authorities conjecture that it may have been $1,500,000,000.[*]

Referring to the table, it is seen that between 1493 and 1660 the production of gold was nearly stationary. The value of the silver product increased about eight-fold between 1493 and 1600, owing to the fabulous yield of the mines of Potosi, in Bolivia, and Pachuca, Zacatecas, and Guanajuato, in Mexico, and the price of silver decreased from $65 per kilogram to $59. During the next 60 years the silver product decreased; but the price of silver, instead of increasing, decreased much more rapidly than in the earlier period.

From 1660 to 1780 the production of silver greatly increased; then rapidly decreased to 1820, and again greatly increased to 1860. The gold product increased from 1660 to 1760, decreased to 1820, and then increased more than tenfold between 1820 and 1860. The relative value of the total production of

---

[*] *Report of Silver Commission,* 1877, p. 8.

gold and silver varied through wide ranges from 1660 to 1860. Notwithstanding these violent fluctuations in both metals, and in the relative product of each, the price of silver per kilogram remained nearly stationary during these 200 years. From 1860 to 1885 the production of gold decreased and that of silver increased, but the great decline in price of silver did not set in until 1873. From a study of these statistics it becomes evident that so long as the production of silver as compared with that of gold fluctuated below the value ratio of the two metals, as established by their coinage values, the value of silver was practically unaffected.

The following table shows the world's production of gold and silver from 1849 to 1889 as given by different authorities. The figures in the columns headed "Soetbeer," from 1853 to 1885, inclusive, are from Dr. Adolph Soetbeer's *Materials toward the Elucidation of the Economic Conditions affecting the Precious Metals*.*

VARIOUS ESTIMATES OF THE WORLD'S PRODUCTION OF GOLD AND SILVER.

Years.	Gold. (Millions of Dollars.)				Silver. (Millions of Dollars.)			
	Soetbeer.	Sir Hector Hay.	Mint Report, 1889.	Most Probable.	Soetbeer. (a).	Sir Hector Hay. (c)	Mint Report, 1889.	Most Probable. (e)
1849			27.1				•39.0	
1850			44.5				39.0	
1851			67.6				40.0	
1852		*82.5	132.8			40.5	40.6	
1853	(b)132.5	155.0	155.5		(b)36.8	40.5	40.6	
1854		127.0	127.5			40.5	40.6	
1855		135.0	135.1	(b)132.5		40.5	40.6	
1856		149.5	147.6	134.0		41.0	40.7	
1857		133.3	133 3	134.0		41.0	40.7	
1858	(b)134.1	124.0	124.7	135 0	(b)37.7	41.0	40.7	
1859		124.5	124.9	130.0		41.0	40.8	
1860		119.0	119.3	127.0		41.5	40.8	(d)40.0
1861		114.0	113.8	122.0		43.0	44.7	45.0
1862		107.0	107.6	119.0		45.5	45.2	46.0
1863	(b)123.0	106.5	107.0	119.0	(b)45.8	49.5	49.2	49.0
1864		113.0	113.0	122.0		52.0	51.7	52.0
1865		120.0	120.2	126.0		52.5	52.0	52.0
1866		121.0	121.1	127.0		52.0	50.8	52.0
1867		116.0	104.0	127.0		50.5	54.2	54.0
1868	(b)129.6	120.0	109.7	126.0	(b)55.7	49.0	50.2	57.0
1869		121.0	106.2	125.0		49.0	47.5	61.0
1870		119.0	106.9	123.0		55.5	51.6	64.0
1871		116.5	107.0	119.0		69.0	61.1	66.0
1872		110.0	99 6	113 0		58.5	65.3	71.0
1873	(b)115.6	111.5	96.2	112.0	(b)81.9	64.0	81.8	75.0
1874		107.5	90.8	111.0		68.0	71.5	79.0
1875		110.5	97.5	111.0		69.0	80 5	82.0
1876	110.3	111.5	103.7	111.0	96.6	77.0	87.6	83.0
1877	119.3	117.0	114.0	116.0	99.3	67.0	81.0	93.0
1878	128.5	110.5	119.0	120.0	106 1	80.5	95.0	97.0
1879	119 2	104 0	109.0	114.0	104 2	79.0	96 0	99.0
1880	108.7	106 0	106.5	108.0	103.1	87.5	96.7	101.0
1881	105.6	103.0	103.0	104.0	107 8	94.0	102.0	106.0
1882	96.7	101.0	102.0	100.0	115 1	102.5	111.8	111.0
1883	96.1	98.0	95 4	97 0	120 4	103.0	115.3	115.0
1884	97.1	95.5	101.7	100.0	122.9	104 0	105.3	120.0
1885	102 7	97.5	108.4	106.0	132.0	106.5	118.5	125.0
1886	107.3		106.0	106.0	134.6		120.6	130.0
1887	106.3		105.8	100 0	141.9		124.3	136.0
1888	106 3		110.2	110.0	151.2		140.7	146.0
1889			121.0	120.0			158.8	159.0

(a) Figured from kilograms at United States coining value. (b) Average for five preceding years. (c) Subsequent to 1873 the figures in this column represent the product of silver calculated at its commercial value. (d) Average for preceding ten years. (e) Based on United States coining value, $1.2929 per oz.

Dr. Soetbeer's figures are in kilograms, and for the table have been reduced to United States coining values by multiplying by $664.61393 per kilogram for gold

* Second edition, Berlin, 1886, translated by Prof. F. W. Taussig, and published in Mr. Edward Atkinson's report of bi metallism in Europe, 1887. (Executive Document 34, Senate, Fiftieth Congress, first session.)

and by $41.56764 per kilogram for silver. The figures in the same column for 1885 to 1888, inclusive, are from Dr. Soetbeer's memoir on the production of gold and silver from 1885 to 1888, presented to the International Monetary Congress at Paris in 1889.

The figures attributed to Sir Hector Hay are from a table furnished by him to the British Commission on " Recent Changes in the Relative Values of the Precious Metals " (1887). His figures, being given in pounds sterling, have been multiplied by five to convert them (approximately) into dollars.

The figures up to 1874 in the columns headed " Mint report" are taken from a table published in the annual report of Hon. Horatio C. Burchard, Director of the United States Mint, on " Production of Gold and Silver in the United States " for 1880, p. 294. The original authority for this table is not given. The close agreement of these figures between 1853 and 1866 with those given by Sir Hector Hay would indicate that both were taken from the same original source for these years. The figures in this column subsequent to 1873 are from the annual report of Hon. Edward O. Leech, Director of the United States Mint, on " Production of Gold and Silver in the United States" for the year 1889, p. 61.

The following estimates of the gold and silver production of the world are taken from the reports of the Director of the United States Mint on the production of gold and silver in the United States. The figures for 1880 are from the report of 1882, those for 1881 from the report of 1884, those for 1882 from the report of 1885, those for 1883 from the report of 1887, those for 1884, 1885, and 1886 from the report of 1888, those for 1887, 1888, and 1889 from the report of 1890, and those for 1890 and 1891 from the report of 1891.

WORLD'S PRODUCTION OF GOLD AND SILVER FROM 1880 TO 1891.

(Kilogram of gold = $604.60. Kilogram of silver = $41.56, coining rate in United States silver dollars.)

Countries.	1880.				1881.			
	Gold.		Silver.		Gold.		Silver.	
	Kilos.	Dollars.	Kilos.	Dollars.	Kilos.	Dollars.	Kilos.	Dollars.
United States........	54.168	36,000,000	942.987	39,200,000	52,212	34,700,000	1,034,649	43,000,000
Australasia....	48,282	28,765,000	5,465	227,125	a46,178	30,690,000	53,970	164,988
Mexico...............	c1,488	989,160	c605,469	25,167,763	d1,293	858,909	d865,918	27,675,540
Russia	c42,960	28,551,028	c11,391	473,519	36,071	24,371,343	7,992	332,198
Germany	e350	232,610	e134,152	5,576,699	f350	232,610	g186,990	7,771,304
Austria-Hungary....	1,647	1,094,596	48,000	1,994,880	1,867	1,240,808	31,359	1,303,280
Sweden.............	5	3,323	1,312	54,527	1	665	1.176	48,875
Norway..			4,436	184,360			4,812	199.987
Italy........	h109	72,375	f432	17,949	j109	72,375	f432	17,949
Spain			74,500	3,096,220			k74,500	3,096,220
Turkey.......... ...	7	4,918	1,719	71,441	7	4,918	1,719	71,441
Canada....	1,226	815,089	1,641	68,205	1,648	1,094,926	1,641	68,205
Argentina ,.........	c118	78.546	c10,109	420,225	l118	78.546	l10,109	420,225
Colombia	c6,019	4,000,000	c24,057	1,000,000	l6,019	4,000,000	l24,057	1,000,000
Bolivia..............	m109	72.345	m264,677	11,000,000	109	72.375	264,677	11,000,000
Chile...............	m194	128,869	m192,275	5,081,747	194	128,869	122,275	5,081,747
Brazil...............	1,345	893,887			1,116	741,804		
Venezuela...........	3,423	2,274,692			k3,423	2,274,692		
Japan...............	c702	466,548	c22,460	916,400	l702	466,548	l22,046	916,400
Africa.	c3,000	1,993,800			g3,000	1,993,800		
Total	160,152	106,436,786	2,275.082	91,551,060	155,016	103,023.078	2,458,322	102,168,354

(*a*) Official for Victoria and New South Wales, with estimated production of the other Provinces. (*b*) The mean of the official production for 1880 and 1882. (*c*) Estimated. (*d*) Coinage and export. (*e*) From total production 17% of gold and 25% of silver deducted for foreign ores. (*f*) Estimated. (*g*) Estimated by Dr. A. Soetbeer. (*h*) Estimated. (*i*) Dr. A. Soetbeer. (*j, k, l, m*) Estimated.

Countries.	1882.				1883.			
	Gold.		Silver.		Gold.		Silver.	
	Kilos.	Dollars.	Kilos.	Dollars.	Kilos.	Dollars.	Kilos.	Dollars.
United States.......	48,902	32,500,000	1,126.063	46,800,000	45,140	30,000,000	1,111,646	46,200,000
Australasia. ..,......	48,081	31,955,017	2,011	83,592	40,852	27,150,000	8,610	150,0(0
Mexico	1,409	936,223	703,508	29,237,798	1,438	956,000	711,460	29,569,000
Russia..............	35,913	23,867,935	7,781	323,427	30,272	20,119,000	9,990	415,000
Germany	376	249,890	214,982	8,934,652	458	304,000	a142,700	5,930,000
Austria-Hungary	b1,580	1,050,068	b47,118	1,958,224	1,638	1,088,000	48,700	2,024,000
Sweden......... ..	17	11,298	1,500	62,350	37	25,000	1,583	66,000
Norway..... .. .	......	......	5,893	244,954	......	......	5,645	235,000
Italy..............	c109	72,375	e432	17,949	d142	94,000	d29,259	1,216,000
Spain	......	......	ef4,500	3,096,230	......	......	f34,335	2,258,000
Turkey.............	10	6,648	2,161	89,916	d10	7,000	d1,323	55,000
France.............	......	......	14,291	594,053	......	......	6,356	264,000
Great Britain......	......	......	......	......	2	1,000	8.500	353,000
Canada.............	g1,648	1,094,926	g1,641	68,205	1,435	954,000	d5,030	209,000
Argentina	h118	78,546	h10,109	420,225	118	78,000	11,500	478,000
Colombia............	5,802	3,856,000	18,283	760,000	i5,802	3,856,000	18,287	760,000
Bolivia.............	g109	72,375	g264,677	11,000,000	109	72,000	384,985	16,000,000
Chile..............	245	168,000	128,106	5,325,000	j500	332,000	j160,000	6,650,000
Brazil..............	g1,116	741,694	......	......	952	633,000	......	......
Venezuela...........	3,904	2,595,077	......	......	5,023	3,338,000	......	......
Peru....	k179	119,250	k45,909	1,908,000	j180	120,000	j45,909	1,908,000
Japan...............	l952	632,520	l21,121	877,772	l290	193,000	l12,940	538,000
Africa	m3,000	1,993,800	......	......	n1,078	717,000	449	19,000
China............. ..	......	......	......	......	o8,057	5,355,000	......	......
Total	153,470	101,996,640	2,690,109	111,802,317	143,583	95,392,000	2,774,227	115,297,000

(a) The production officially reported with a deduction of 68,000 kilograms, given by Dr. Soetbeer for 1884 as the amount from foreign ores smelted. (b) Official for Hungary, with former annual production for Austria added. (c, d, e) Estimated. (f) Estimate of Dr. Soetbeer for 1883. (g, h, i, j, k, l) Estimated. (m) Estimated by Dr. A. Soetbeer, 1879. (n) From Board of Trade returns by A. Sauerbeck. (o) Dr. Ivan C. Michels.

Countries.	1884.				1885.			
	Gold.		Silver.		Gold.		Silver.	
	Kilos.	Dollars.	Kilos.	Dollars.	Kilos.	Dollars.	Kilos.	Dollars.
United States.......	46,344	30,800,000	1,174,206	48,800,000	47,848	31,800,000	1,241,578	51,600,000
Australasia.........	42,558	28,284,000	4,525	188,000	41,287	a27,439,000	25,220	1,048,000
Mexico	1,780	1,183,000	655,870	27,258,000	1,304	867,000	772,670	32,112,000
Russia.............	32,913	21,874,000	9,360	389,000	38,125	25,338,000	15,550	646,000
Germany	555	369,000	27,598	1,147,000	1,378	916,000	24,567	1,021,000
Austria-Hungary ...	1,658	1,102,000	49,300	2,049,000	1,774	1,179,000	52,748	2,192,000
Sweden....	20	13,000	1,816	75,500	47	31,000	2,326	96,000
Norway....	......	......	6,387	265,500	......	......	7,200	299,000
Italy ,.............	b195	122,600	b33,639	1,406,350	b195	129,800	b33,639	1,406,350
Spain	......	......	c54,335	2,258,000	......	......	c54,335	2,258,000
Turkey.............	b10	7,000	b1,323	55,000	b10	7,000	b1,323	55,000
France.............	......	......	5,905	245,000	......	......	51,000	2,120,000
Great Britain	......	......	8,060	335,000	......	......	7,607	316,000
Canada.............	d1,435	954,000	55,030	200,000	1,679	1,116,000	b5,030	209,000
Argentina ;........	d118	78,000	d11,500	478,000	d118	78,000	d11,500	478,000
Colombia...........	e5,802	3,856,000	e18,287	760,000	b3,762	2,500,000	b9,525	400,000
Bolivia.............	d109	72,000	f240,616	10,000,000	d109	72,000	f240,616	10,000,000
Chile	500	332,000	160,000	6,650,000	b500	332,000	b210,000	8,727,600
Brazil..............	d952	633,000	......	......	..204	800,000	2,640	110,000
Venezuela	g7,033	4,674,000	......	......	7,033	4,674,000	......	......
Peru...............	180	120,000	45,909	1,908,000	228	150,000	47,840	1,988,000
Central America	......	......	......	......	9	6,000	......	......
Japan	296	197,000	23,460	975,000	265	176,000	23,065	960,000
Africa	g1,250	830,000	h258	10,000	h2,063	1,384,000	h1,274	53,000
China.............	i9,302	6,222,000	......	......	i6,997	4,650,000	......	......
India (British)......	... ..	....	....	....	203	135,000	....	....
Total....	158,070	101,729,600	2,537,564	105,461,350	156,156	103,779,600	2,841,573	118,095,150

(a) G. W. Griffin, United States consul at Sydney, reports gold of Australasia, 1886, at $25,883,884, and 1385 at $27,361,603. (b) Estimated. (c) Estimate of Dr. Soetbeer for 1883. (d, e) Estimated. (f) Estimated upon annual average credited Bolivia by Dr. A. Soetbeer, and official statistics of exports and coinage for 1887. (g) Estimated. (h) Board of Trade returns by A. Sauerbeck. (i) Dr. Ivan C. Michels.

Countries.	1886.				1887.			
	Gold.		Silver.		Gold.		Silver.	
	Kilos.	Dollars.	Kilos.	Dollars.	Kilos.	Dollars.	Kilos.	Dollars.
United States.......	52,663	85,000,000	1,227,141	51,000,000	49,654	83,000,000	1,283,855	53,897,000
Australasia........	39,761	a26,425,000	29,403	1,222,000	41,119	27,327,600	6,422	266,900
Mexico	924	614,000	794,033	33,000,000	1,240	824,000	904,000	37,570,000
Russia............	30,872	20,518,000	12,707	528,100	30,232	20,092,000	13,522	562,000
Germany......... ..	1,065	708,000	25,050	1,066,000	2,251	1,496,000	31,564	1,811,798
Austria-Hungary...	b1,774	1,179,000	552,746	2,192,200	1,877	1,247,450	53,391	2,218,900
Sweden	67	45,000	3,081	128,000	84	55,550	c5,828	242,250
Norway............			b7,200	299,000			d5,147	214,000
Italy...............	.195	129,600	33,839	1,406,350	c195	129,000	c33,839	1,406,320
Spain............			e54,335	2,258,000			58,711	2,440,000
Turkey ....,	10	7,000	1,323	55,000	c10	7,000	c1,323	55,000
France			46,789	1,944,550			54,314	2,257,300
Great Britain......			10,124	420,750		1,000	9,964	414,100
Canada............	2,003	1,330,442	5,030	209,000	1,773	1,178,637	10,868	451,680
Argentina.........	30	20,000	1,444	60,000	45	30,000	722	30,000
Colombia..........	3,762	2,500,000	9,625	400,000	4,514	3,000,000	24,061	1,000,000
Bolivia............	f109	72,000	g240,616	10,000,000	143	95,000	137,468	5,713,170
Chile.............	500	332,000	210,000	8,727,600	2,379	1,581,400	199,516	8,291,020
Brazil.	h1,502	998,000	h141	5,850	984	654,000		
Venezuela..........	i5,020	3,336,000			.2,960	1,967,216		
Guiana (British)...					370	245,002		
Guiana (Dutch).....					712	j473,000		
Peru	k170	113,000	k95,246	4,000,000	d158	105,000	175,263	3,128,000
Central America	m131	87,000			226	n150,000	48,123	n2,000,000
Japan.............	492	327,235	32,242	1,340,000	564	375,000	32,065	1,332,650
Africa.............	o2,103	1,438,000	3,165	132,000	2,868	1,910,600	432	17,900
China.............	p5,492	3,650,000			p14,204	9,500,000		
India (British)......	634	421,600			481	320,000		
Total	149,338	99,250,877	2,896,882	120,394,400	159,155	105,774,955	2,990,398	124,280,974

(a) G. W. Griffin, United States consul at Sydney, reports the gold production of Australasia for 1886 at $25,883,884, and for 1885 at $27,361,603. (b, c, d) Estimated. (e) Estimate of Dr. Soetbeer for 1883. (f) Estimated. (g) Estimate based upon the annual average credited Bolivia by Dr. A. Soetbeer and official statistics of exports and coinage for 1887. (h) Exports of gold and silver through the custom-house at Rio de Janeiro. (i) Production of two mills of the El Callao Company. (j) *Jaarcijifers over 1888 en Vorige Jaaren*, No. 8, p. 115. (k, l, m, n) Estimated. (o) Board of Trade returns by A. Sauerbeck. (p) Imports of gold into Great Britain from China.

Countries.	1888.				1889.			
	Gold.		Silver.		Gold.		Silver.	
	Kilos.	Dollars.	Kilos.	Dollars.	Kilos.	Dollars.	Kilos.	Dollars.
United States.......	49,917	33,175,000	1,424,326	59,195,000	49,353	32,800,000	1,555,486	64,646,000
Australasia	42,974	28,560,660	120,308	a5,000,000	49,784	33,086,700	144,369	a6,000,000
Mexico	1,465	974,000	995,500	41,373,000	1,053	700,000	1,335,828	55,517,000
Russia..........	32,052	21,302,000	14,523	604,000	34,867	23,173,000	14,389	598,000
Germany..........	1,792	1,190,963	32,051	1,332,024	1,958	1,301,286	32,040	1,331,576
Austria-Hungary....	1,820	1,209,572	52,128	2,166,440	2,198	1,461,000	52,651	2,188,000
Sweden	76	50,000	4,648	163,000	74	48,900	4,267	177,400
Norway			5,147	214,000			5,147	214,000
Italy..........	148	98,000	35	1,454	b148	98,000	b35	1,454
Spain			51,502	2,140,400			b51,502	2,140,400
Turkey	c10	7,000	c1,323	55,000	10	7,000	c1,323	55,000
France			49,396	2,053,000			b49,396	2,053,000
Great Britain.......	220	146,000	9,047	376,000	97	64,370	9,522	395,734
Canada............	1,673	1,111,959	9,264	385,000	1,919	1,275,045	b9,264	385,000
Argentina..........	47	31,000	10,226	425,000	b47	31,000	b10,226	425,000
Colombia...........	4,514	3,000,000	24,061	1,000,000	3,762	2,500,000	31,280	1,300,000
Bolivia............	90	59,800	230,460	9,578,000	b90	59,800	b230,460	9,578,000
Chile...	2,953	1,962,430	183,851	7,723,937	2,164	1,436,600	123,695	5,140,764
Brazil..............	670	445,800			670	b445,800		
Venezuela..........	2,130	1,415,598			2,765	1,838,000		
Guiana (British)....	450	.299,070			882	586,177		
Guiana (Dutch)......	487	d324,000			487	324,000		
Peru................	158	105,000	75,263	3,128,000	140	93,044	68,575	2,850,000
Central America	226	e150,000	48,123	e2,000,000	226	e150,000	48,123	e2,000,000
Japan	f606	403,000	f42,424	1,763,140	f606	403,000	f42,424	1,763,140
Africa	6,771	4,500,000			12,920	8,5-6,63?		
China.	g13,542	9,000,000			13,542	69,000,000		
India (British)	1,018	676,563			2,261	1,502,660		
Total	165,809	110,196,915	3,385,606	140,706,413	182,021	120,971,514	3,820,002	158,759,468

(a, b, c) Estimated. (d) *Jaareijifers over 1888 en Vorige Jaaren*, No. 8, p. 115. (e) Estimated. (f) Product of private mines in 1888; Government mines in 1889. (g) Imports of gold into Great Britain and British India from China.

Countries.	1890.				1891.			
	Gold.		Silver.		Gold.		Silver.	
	Kilos.	Dollars.	Kilos.	Dollars.	Kilos.	Dollars.	Kilos.	Dollars.
United States.......	49,421	32,845,000	1,895,800	70,465,000	49,917	33,175,000	1,814,642	75,416,500
Australasia........	44,851	29,508,000	288,212	10,731,300	47,245	31,809,000	311,100	12,929,800
Mexico............	1,154	707,000	1,211,646	50,356,000	1,505	1,000,000	1,275,265	53,000,000
Russia............	38,345	25,484,000	3,326	138,200	38,310	24,131,500	13,847	575,500
Germany..........	....	....	182,086	7,567,500	....	....	a180,000	7,480,500
Austria-Hungary....	2,104	1,308,500	50,613	2,103,500	e2,104	1,308,500	e50,613	2,103,500
Sweden...........	58	58,500	4,160	173,700	e88	58,500	e4,160	173,700
Norway...........	....	....	5,530	230,200	....	....	e5,539	230,200
Italy.............	f150	100,000	i8,108	337,000	f150	100,000	i8,108	337,000
Spain.............	....	....	c51,502	2,140,400	....	....	c51,502	2,140,400
Turkey...........	d10	7,000	d1,323	55,000	d10	7,000	d1,323	55,000
France...........	200	133,000	71,117	2,055,000	e200	133,000	e71,117	2,055,600
Great Britain.......	4	3,000	9,075	377,200	4	e3,000	9,075	c377,200
Canada...........	2,508	1,606,000	12,464	518,000	2,500	e1,606,000	12,464	e518,000
Argentina..........	123	82,000	14,680	610,100	e123	82,000	14,680	e610,100
Colombia..........	5,416	3,600,000	19,971	830,000	5,224	3,472,000	31,232	1,298,000
Bolivia............	101	67,000	301,112	12,514,200	e101	67,000	372,866	15,488,000
Chile.............	b2,162	1,436,600	b123,696	5,140,800	b2,162	1,486,600	72,185	a3,000,000
Brazil............	670	c445,300	....	....	670	c445,300	....	....
Venezuela.........	2,512	1,670,000	....	....	1,504	1,000,000	....	....
Guiana (British)....	1,693	1,125,000	....	....	e1,693	1,125,000	....	....
Guiana (Dutch)....	668	441,200	....	....	668	e444,200	....	....
Guiana (French)....	f725	548,000	....	....	f825	548,000	....	....
Peru	104	69,000	65,701	2,734,300	113	75,000	74,879	3,112,000
Uruguay..........	140	93,500	....	....	140	e93,500	....	....
Central America ...	226	g150,000	48,123	g2,100,000	226	g150,000	48,123	g2,000,000
Japan.............	764	507,700	42,408	1,785,000	775	515,000	43,282	1,798,800
Africa............	14,877	9,887,000	....	....	21,366	14,199,600	....	....
China............	h8,020	5,330,000	....	....	e8,020	5,330,000	....	....
India (British)......	3,009	2,000,000	....	....	3,754	2,495,000	....	....
Corea...........	1,128	750,000	....	....	1,128	e750,000	....	....
Total...........	181,271	120,475,300	4,180,532	173,743,000	186,531	125,299,700	4,465,822	185,599,600

(*a, b, c, d, e, f, g*) Estimated. (*h*) Imports of gold bullion from China into London and India. (*i*) Estimated.

COMMERCIAL RATIO OF SILVER TO GOLD EACH YEAR SINCE 1687.

(From 1687 to 1832 the ratios are taken from Dr. A. Soetbeer; from 1833 to 1878 from Pixley and Abell's tables; and for subsequent years from daily cablegrams from London to the Bureau of the Mint.)

Year.	Ratio.	Year.	Ratio.	Year.	Ratio.	Year.	Ratio.	Year.	Ratio.	Year.	Ratio.
1687 ...	14.94	1722....	15.17	1757	14.87	1792....	15.17	1827....	15.74	1862 ...	15.35
1688....	14.04	1723....	15.20	1758....	14.85	1793	15.00	1828....	15.78	1863...	15.37
1689....	15.02	1724....	15.11	1759....	14.15	1794....	15.37	1829....	15.78	1864....	15.37
1690....	15.02	1725....	15.11	1760....	14.14	1795....	15.55	1830....	15.82	1865...	15.44
1691....	14.98	1726....	15.15	1761....	14.54	1796....	15.65	1831....	15.72	1866 ...	15.43
1692....	14.92	1727....	15.24	1762 ...	15.27	1797....	15.41	1832....	15.73	1867...	15.57
1693 ...	14.83	1728....	15.11	1763....	14.99	1798....	15 59	1833....	15.93	1868...	15.59
1694....	14.87	1729....	14.92	1764....	14.70	1799....	15.74	1834....	15.73	1869...	15.60
1695....	15.02	1730....	14.61	1765....	14.83	1800....	15.68	1835....	15.80	1870 ...	15.57
1696....	15.00	1731....	14.94	1766....	14.80	1801....	15.46	1836....	15.72	1871...	15.57
1697....	15.20	1732....	15.09	1767....	14.85	1802....	15.26	1837....	15.83	1872...	15.63
1698....	15.07	1733....	15.18	1768....	14.80	1803....	15.41	1838....	15.85	1873...	15.92
1699....	14.94	1734....	15.39	1769....	14.72	1804....	15.41	1839....	15.62	1874....	16.17
1700....	14.81	1735....	15.41	1770....	14.62	1805....	15.79	1840....	15.62	1875....	16.59
1701....	15.07	1736....	15.18	1771....	14.66	1806....	15.52	1841....	15.70	1876....	17.88
1702....	15.52	1737....	15.02	1772 ...	14.52	1807....	15.43	1842 ...	15.87	1877....	17.22
1703....	15.17	1738....	14.91	1773....	14.62	1808....	16.08	1843....	15.93	1878...	17.94
1704....	15.22	1739....	14.91	1774....	14.62	1809....	15.96	1844....	15 85	1879...	18.40
1705....	15.11	1740....	14.94	1775....	14.72	1810....	15.77	1845....	15.92	1880....	18.05
1706....	15.27	1741....	14.92	1776....	14.55	1811....	15.53	1846....	15.90	1881...	18.16
1707....	15.44	1742....	14.85	1777....	14.54	1812....	16.11	1847....	15.80	1882...	18.19
1708....	15.41	1743....	14.85	1778....	14.66	1813....	16.25	1848....	15.85	1883...	18 64
1709....	15.31	1744....	14.87	1779....	14.80	1814....	15.04	1849....	15 78	1884...	18.67
1710....	15.22	1745....	14.98	1780....	14.72	1815....	15.26	1850....	15 70	1885...	19.41
1711....	15.29	1746....	15.13	1781....	14.78	1816....	15.28	1851....	15.46	1886...	20.78
1712 ..	15.31	1747....	15.26	1782....	14.42	1817....	15.11	1852....	15.59	1887...	21.13
1713 ...	15.24	1748....	15.11	1783....	14.48	1818....	15.35	1853....	15.33	1888...	21.99
1714....	15.13	1749....	14.80	1784....	14.70	1819....	15.33	1854....	15.33	1889...	22.10
1715....	15.11	1750....	14.55	1785....	14.92	1820....	15.62	1855....	15.38	1890...	19.76
1716....	15.09	1751....	14.39	1786....	14.96	1821....	15.95	1856....	15.36	1891...	20.92
1717....	15.13	1752....	14.54	1787....	14.92	1822....	15 80	1857....	15.27	1892. .	23.73
1718....	15.11	1753....	14.54	1788....	14.85	1823....	15.84	1858....	15.38		
1719....	15.09	1754....	14.48	1789....	14.75	1824....	15.82	1859....	15.19		
1720....	15.04	1755....	14.68	1790....	15.04	1825....	15.70	1860....	15.29		
1721....	15.05	1756....	14.94	1791....	15.05	1826 ...	15.76	1861....	15.50		

General Statistics.

The total coinage of silver dollars under Act of Feb. 28, 1878, was $378,166,793; under Act of July 14, 1890, $34,631,720; under Act of March 3, 1891, trade-dollar bullion, $5,078,472; grand total to Dec. 31, 1892, $417,876,985. The purchases of fine silver by the United States sinceFeb. 12, 1873, were us follows:

Act February 12, 1873	5,434,282 ounces.	Cost, $ 7,152,564	Average price, $1.314
" January 14, 1875	31,603,906 "	" 37,571,148	" " 1.159
" February 28, 1878	291,202,019 "	" 308,199,262	" " 1.058
" July 11, 1890, to December 1, 1892	129,779,322 "	" 124,652,429	" " 0 96
Totals	458,109,529	$477,575,408	$1.0425

The amount of gold used in the industrial arts in the United States in 1892 was, according to the Director of the Mint, $19,329,000, of which $10,588,703 was new bullion. The amount of silver used was $9,350,000 (coining value), of which $7,204,210 (coining value) represented new bullion. The total metallic stock on January 1, 1893, was estimated as: Gold, $649,788,020; silver, $593,365,365; total, $1,243,153,385. The stock of gold in the United States fell off during the year 1892 $39,000,000, while the stock of silver increased $46,000,000. The amount of money in circulation (exclusive of the amount in the Treasury) was $1,611,321,753 on January 1, 1893, an increase of $18,928,124 during the year.

HIGHEST, LOWEST, AND AVERAGE PRICE OF SILVER IN NEW YORK AND LONDON IN 1892.*

Month.	Highest.	Lowest.	Average Price per Ounce, British Standard, .925.	Equivalent Value of a Fine Ounce with Exchange at Par, $4.8065.	Average Monthly Price at New York of Exchange on London.	Eq'vt of Fine oz. based on Monthly Price and Average Rate of Exchange.	Average Monthly New York Price of Fine Bar Silver.
	Pence.	Pence.	Pence.				
January	43 1/4	41 1/4	42.830	$0.92888	$4.8525	$0.93515	$0.93494
February	41 13/16	41 1/8	41.460	.90885	4.8754	.91106	.91198
March	41 5/8	39	40.087	.87875	4.8775	.89699	.89907
April	40 1/8	39 1/4	39.703	.86583	4.8417	.87229	.87379
May	40 3/8	39 11/16	40.060	.87816	4.8788	.88029	.88120
June	41 1/8	40 1/16	40.564	.88921	4.8839	.89298	.89430
July	40 3/16	39 1/16	39.632	.86877	4.8833	.87181	.87270
August	39 5/16	37 1/8	38.295	.83947	4.8812	.84203	.84163
September	38 9/16	38 1/8	38.159	.83646	4.8751	.83601	.84010
October	39 3/8	38 1/8	38.937	.85354	4.8628	.85387	.85740
November	39 1/4	38 1/4	38.971	.85428	4.8703	.85512	.85614
December	39 1/8	37 15/16	38.346	.84058	4.8793	.84274	.84000
Average			39.753	.87106	4.8717	.87427	.87552

* Compiled by the Director of the Mint.

HIGHEST, LOWEST, AND AVERAGE PRICE OF BAR-SILVER IN LONDON.

[Per ounce British standard (0.925), since 1833, and the equivalent in United States gold coin of an ounce 1000 fine, taken at the average price.]

Years.	Lowest.	Highest.	Average.	Average.	Years.	Lowest.	Highest.	Average.	Average.
	Pence.	Pence.	Pence.			Pence.	Pence.	Pence.	
1833	58.750	59.875	59.188	$1.297	1863	61.000	61.750	61.375	$1.345
1834	59.750	60.750	59.938	1.313	1864	60.625	62.500	61.375	1.345
1835	59.250	60.000	59.688	1.308	1865	60.500	61.625	61.063	1.338
1836	59.625	60.375	60.000	1.315	1866	60.375	62.250	61.125	1.339
1837	59.000	60.375	59.563	1.305	1867	60.375	61.250	60.563	1.328
1838	59.500	60.125	59.500	1.304	1868	60.125	61.125	60.500	1.326
1839	60.000	60.625	60.375	1.323	1869	60.000	61.000	60.438	1.325
1840	60.125	60.750	60.375	1.323	1870	60.250	60.750	60.563	1.328
1841	59.750	60.375	60.063	1.316	1871	60.188	61.000	60.500	1.326
1842	59.250	60.000	59.438	1.303	1872	59.250	61.125	60.813	1.322
1843	59.000	59.625	59.188	1.297	1873	57.875	59.938	59.250	1.298
1844	59.250	59.750	59.500	1.304	1874	57.250	59.500	58.313	1.278
1845	58.875	59.875	59.250	1.298	1875	55.500	57.625	56.875	1.246
1846	59.000	60.125	59.813	1.300	1876	46.750	58.500	52.750	1.156
1847	58.875	60.375	59.688	1.308	1877	53.250	58.250	54.813	1.201
1848	58.500	60.000	59.500	1.304	1878	49.500	55.250	52.563	1.152
1849	59.500	60.000	59.750	1.309	1879	48.875	53.750	51.250	1.123
1850	59.500	61.500	61.063	1.316	1880	51.625	52.875	52.250	1.145
1851	60.000	61.625	61.000	1.337	1881	50.875	52.875	51.938	1.138
1852	59.875	61.875	60.500	1.326	1882	50.000	52.875	51.813	1.136
1853	60.625	61.875	61.500	1.348	1883	50.000	51.188	50.625	1.110
1854	60.875	61.875	61.500	1.348	1884	49.500	51.375	50.750	1.113
1855	60.000	61.625	61.313	1.344	1885	46.875	50.000	48.563	1.065
1856	60.500	62.250	61.313	1.344	1886	42.000	47.000	45.375	0.995
1857	61.000	62.375	61.750	1.353	1887	43.250	47.125	44.625	0.978
1858	60.750	61.875	61.313	1.344	1888	41.625	44.563	42.875	0.940
1859	61.750	62.750	62.063	1.360	1889	42.000	44.375	42.688	0.936
1860	61.250	62.375	61.688	1.352	1890	43.625	54.625	47.750	1.046
1861	60.125	61.375	60.813	1.333	1891	43.500	48.750	45.063	0.988
1862	61.000	62.125	61.438	1.346	1892	37.875	43.750	39.813	0.876

COINAGES OF NATIONS.*

	1887 Gold	1887 Silver	1888 Gold	1888 Silver	1889 Gold	1889 Silver	1890 Gold	1890 Silver	1891 Gold	1891 Silver
United States	$23,972,383	$35,191,081	$31,380,808	$33,025,606	$21,413,931	$35,496,683	$20,467,182	$39,202,908	$29,222,005	$27,518,856
Mexico	398,647	29,844,031	800,480	20,656,964	319,907	25,294,726	284,059	24,061,102	250,565	24,483,071
Great Britain	9,728,498	4,142,136	9,883,575	3,661,886	36,502,536	10,927,692	37,375,479	6,352,232	32,720,633	5,141,594
Australia	24,122,267		24,415,220		28,325,529		25,702,600		36,988,044	
India (a)	4,240	44,142,013	104,216	36,297,132	110,326	37,887,814		57,031,333	117,411	52,070,498
Canada		85,000		247,174		16,585		38,000		300,000
France	4,760,960	1,518,742	106,949	1,114,379	3,373,215	71	3,976,340		3,362,450	
Cochin China		3,128,410		1,100,518		1,302,581				
Monaco									388,000	
Belgium		568,632	469,750	16,714	386,000	60,208	263,829	1,081	250,000	150,000
Italy		6,253,900	16,984	62,483		217,125	482,500	279,650	396,000	11,351,000
Switzerland		270,900		1,163,198	3,378,631	4,716,029	9,049,569	1,479,182	250,000	7,277,040
Spain	270,000	11,388,414	102,000	74,448	96,120	680,400	407,160	540,000	199,350	395,000
Portugal	163,831	960,120	143,051		623,943	139,660		198,990		
Netherlands		70,380		4,496,804						
Germany	29,135,470	715,343	34,940,722	989,127	46,166,245	177,079	28,835,512	3,857,118	14,277,220	1,130,282
Austria-Hungary (b)	2,669,750	5,596,385	2,747,633	5,516,190	3,291,067	4,526,250	2,818,750	120,600	2,485,561	3,035,730
Norway		80,400		53,500		53,600		253,987		55,000
Sweden		56,068		16,714		142,253				20,000
Denmark	314,890		20,460,491	62,483		27,607	883,432	547,931	2,110,981	122,698
Russia (c)	20,109,276		66,000	1,163,198	1,060,040	142,253	21,726,289		3,386,000	2,690,932
Turkey		1,551,710		74,448	18,865,097	1,153,651	44,840	1,614,422		221,000
Siam										
Egypt	246,354	2,916,065	257,154	8,463		1,446,636	1,194,050	7,296,645	1,063,725	822,466
Japan	807,420	2,159,690	674,335	10,222,108	1,775,010	9,518,359		300,000		8,523,901
Tunis		10,270,555						881,996		675,500
Chile	25,300	500,000	42,170	132,375					2,663,400	
Argentina	9,173,370	393,000	8,316,825	3,258,000		2,842,531		2,687,119		
Peru				600,443		216,136				
Colombia		1,685,000	660,500	272,000						81,125
Venezuela		663,008	26,082	868,355			86,023			
Brazil								73,136		
Honduras		71,978						1,078		
Congo		19,300						6,436		
German East Africa								607,814		630,000
Great Comoro								28,951		
French Colonies										
Eritrea (Italian Colony)										
British Africa										
British West Indies										23,000
Nicaragua		400,000		244,000						
Straits Settlements		177,000				300,000				398,000
Hawaiian Islands										
Ecuador										
Hongkong		400,000		473,177		1,100,000		450,000		1,500,000
Costa Rica				1,105,000						
Bolivia		1,768,451		1,768,452		258,010		888,000		1,275,385

* From Director of the Mint's report. (h) Silver florin calculated at coining rate, $0.462. (c) Silver ruble calculated at coining rate, $0.7718.
(a) Rupee calculated at coining rate, $0.473r.
NOTE.—The following produced in 1891 only: Silver: China, $4,854,187; Morocco, $290,898; Zanzibar, $60,000; San Domingo, $183,330. Gold: South African Republic, $75,000.

CHRONOLOGY OF THE GOLD AND SILVER INDUSTRY, 1442-1892.

BY WALTER RENTON INGALLS.

The following chronology, compiled from various authorities, forms a brief history of the gold and silver mining industry for a period of 450 years, together with a record of the changes in the monetary position of the two metals. The dates given are believed to be in the main accurate, and are of interest in connection with the statistical tables of production.

1442: Gonçales Baldeza returned from a voyage to regions about Bojador, West Africa, bringing with him the first gold from the western coast of that continent.

1471: The silver mines at Schneeberg, Saxony, were first worked; up to 1500 the yield is estimated to have been more than 160 tons (163,000 kilos) of silver, but after that year the output decreased rapidly.

1492: Discovery of America by Columbus, whose chief object of search was gold, which he found in considerable quantity among the natives of the islands he reached.

1516: The silver mines at Joachimsthal, Bohemia, were in flourishing condition at the beginning of the sixteenth century. In 1516 some 8000 miners were employed there.

1521: Conquest of Mexico by Hernando Cortés.

1522: The first silver sent to Europe from the mines of Mexico was obtained from Tasco, discovered by the Spaniards this year. These mines together with those of Pachuca are considered the oldest in Mexico, some of them having been long worked by the Aztecs at the time of the arrival of the Spaniards.

1527: There are no documents to show when silver-mining was first begun at Przibram, Bohemia, but, according to the municipal records, a concession to reopen the mines was granted in 1527.

1532: Conquest of Peru by Francisco Pizarro.

1537: Gold-mining was begun by the Spaniards in New Granada (United States of Colombia).

1540: Work was begun by the Spaniards in the silver mines of Zacatecas, Mexico.

1545: Discovery of the famous silver mines of Potosí, Bolivia.

1548: First discovery of silver at Guanajuato, Mexico.

1555: The silver mines at Sombrerete, Zacatecas, Mexico, began to produce.

1557: Invention of the patio process of silver amalgamation by Bartolomé de Medina, of Pachuca, Mexico.

1571: The Huancevalica quicksilver mines in Peru first began to produce in noteworthy quantity. This was an important event, as an abundant supply of mercury for the amalgamation of Potosí ore was thereby obtained.

1574: The patio process was introduced in Peru.

1575: Discovery of the silver mines of Oruro, Bolivia.

1577: The placers of Brazil were first discovered this year, but they were not actively worked until 1674, and their product did not begin to be important until 1695.

1590: Invention of the system of copper-pan or "cazo" amalgamation by Alonzo Barba, at Potosí, Bolivia.

1609: Holland maintained from 1609 to 1816 a silver monetary standard, giving gold a nominal valuation at a ratio of 14.7 to 1.

1623: Discovery of silver at Kongsberg, Norway; the works at that place were established the same year.

1630: Discovery of the famous silver mines of Cerro de Pasco, Peru.

1632: Discovery of the silver mines of Batopilas, Chihuahua, Mexico.

1633: Invention of the aludel furnace for the reduction of quicksilver, by L. S. Barba, a Peruvian; this was the first efficient furnace devised for this purpose.

1666: Discovery of the silver mines of Cusihuiriachic, Chihuahua, Mexico.

1688: Silver was the legal measure of value in Hamburg, a city of extensive commerce, from 1688 until recent times, but gold also was coined at a ratio of $14\frac{4}{5}$ to 1.

1695: The rich placers of Minas Geraes, Brazil, began to produce largely.

1702: Establishment of the school of mines at Freiberg, Saxony.

1704: Discovery of the silver mines of Santa Eulalia, Chihuahua, Mexico. Discovery of silver at Nertschinsk, Siberia, and the first regular mining of precious metals in that country was begun.

1710: The metallurgical works at Freiberg, Saxony, were established.

1717: From 1717 to 1816, the legal ratio between gold and silver in England was $15\frac{1}{2}$ to 1.

1737: Discovery of gold near Voitsk, Government of Archangel, Russia.

1745: Important discovery of gold-bearing quartz on the Beriozofsk River, near Ekaterinburg, in the Ural, Russia. Gold-mining was also commenced on Snake Mountain, in the Altai Range, Siberia.

1762: Discovery of the great silver bonanza of Real del Monte, Mexico.

1771: Discovery of the rich silver mines of Hualgayo, Peru.

1774: The first placers in the Ural were discovered this year, quartz lodes having been opened nearly thirty years previous.

1778: The silver mines of Catorce, Mexico, were opened and proved to be rich.

1783: Zambrano discovered the famous silver mines of Guarisamey, Durango, Mexico.

1786: Prior to the Constitution of 1789, the Congress of the American States had, in 1786, established a double monetary standard with a ratio of $15\frac{1}{4}$ to 1, fixing as unit the dollar of pure silver of 375.64 grains.

1790: Barrel amalgamation was introduced at the metallurgical works at Freiberg, Saxony.

1792: The famous bonanza at Sombrerete, Zacatecas, Mexico, was discovered this year, the mines at that place having been worked for more than two centuries.

The legal ratio between gold and silver in the United States was made 15 to 1, by the act of Congress creating a mint.

1793: Mules and horses were used in Mexico, for the first time, for mixing the pulp, mercury, and chemicals in the patio process, saving 75% in the cost of this branch of working; prior to this time, the operation had been performed entirely by human labor.

1798: Discovery of the great bonanza (silver) at Ramos, Mexico.

1803: France adopted the double monetary standard at a ratio of $15\frac{1}{2}$ to 1;

previous to the Revolution, the ratio between gold and silver in that country had been 15 to 1.

1805: The gold mines of the Ancosta district, Bolivia, commenced to yield.

1810: Discovery of silver at El Refugio, Chihuahua, Mexico.

1816: Discovery of the Melkowa placers, Siberia.

England adopted the gold standard by act of Parliament of this year.

Silver was the sole standard in Holland until this year, when the double standard was adopted at a ratio of 15.873 to 1.

1821: Resumption of specie payments in gold by the Bank of England.

1824: Discovery of silver at Palmarejo, Chihuahua, Mexico.

The silver mines of Fresnillo, Zacatecas, Mexico, were opened.

1829: Discovery of gold mines in Georgia; first mining excitement in the United States.

1830: Discovery of the placers of the Altai Mountains, Siberia.

Discovery of the silver mines of Guadalcañal, Spain.

1832: The silver mines of Chañarcillo, near Copiapo, Chile, were opened.

1834: The legal ratio between gold and silver in the United States was made 16 to 1.

1837: The St. John del Rey Mining Company, operating the Morro Velho gold mine in Brazil, commenced to produce largely.

1839: Count Strzelecki is said to have found gold in New South Wales in 1839, but in deference to the wishes of the Governor, Sir G. Phipps, the discovery was kept secret, the colony being then a penal one. In 1841, Rev. W. Clark also found gold, and in 1847 he called the attention of the colonists to the auriferous character of the country. The value of the diggings was not realized, however, until Hargreaves made his discovery in 1851.

1843: The Augustin process of working silver ores was introduced at the Gottesbelohnung Hütte, near Mansfeld, Germany, and later in the year at the Freiberg works.

Discovery of the silver mines of Hien de la Encina, in Guadalajara, Spain.

1847: Holland again adopted the silver standard.

1848: On January 19, Marshall discovered gold at Coloma, Cal. This find started the rush of gold-seekers to the Pacific Coast, and by the end of the year numerous discoveries of the precious metal had been made in various portions of the State, notably along the American and Feather rivers.

The Ziervogel process for treating silver ores was introduced at Freiberg, superseding the Augustin process.

1849: Discovery of gold in the bed of the Yuruari River, Venezuela, but the region did not become the scene of great operations until several years later.

Discovery of gold in Gold Cañon, Nevada; an important event, as it eventually led to the discovery of the Comstock lode.

1850: Belgium adopted the single silver monetary standard.

Quartz-mining was begun in California.

1851: Discovery of gold in New South Wales by Hargreaves.

Discovery of gold at Ballarat and Bendigo, in Victoria, following close upon the discoveries in New South Wales.

Work was begun at the quicksilver mines of New Almaden, California.

1852: Discovery of gold in South Australia and Tasmania.

Invention of the process of hydraulic mining in California by Edward E. Mattison, a native of Connecticut.

1857: Discovery of gold in New Zealand.

Suspension of specie payments by Russia.

The German States, including Austria, adopted a single silver standard.

1858: Discovery of gold at Canoona, Queensland.

The Patera process was introduced at Joachimsthal, Bohemia; the use of sodium hyposulphite as a lixiviant for silver ores having been first suggested by Dr. Percy in 1848.

1859: The Comstock lode, Nevada, was discovered early in the year by O'Reilly and McLaughlin, at the point where the Ophir mine is located. The Grosh brothers found silver in this vicinity several years previous, but their discovery came to naught.

Discovery of gold in the Fraser River region, British Columbia.

Pike's Peak excitement; discovery of gold placers in Gilpin County, Colorado, in California Gulch, and at Breckenridge.

1860: Invention of the Washoe process of pan amalgamation by Almarin B. Paul and James Smith.

Discovery of the Gould & Curry and Savage bonanzas in the Comstock lode.

Discovery of the placers of the Boisé Basin in Idaho.

After seventeen centuries of neglect the silver-lead mines of Laurium, in Greece, were reopened, a French company having obtained a concession of the property.

1861: Belgium returned to the double monetary standard.

Discovery of gold in Nova Scotia.

Discovery of rich placers in Oregon.

1862: Suspension of specie payments by the United States.

First important discoveries of gold in Montana.

Discovery of silver in the Reese River district, Nevada.

1863: First discoveries of argentiferous lead ores in Little Cottonwood Cañon, Utah.

1864: First locations at Eureka, Nevada, but no important discoveries (silver-lead) were made until the fall of 1869. Claims were also located at Pioche, in the same State, though operations at that place did not become successful until several years later.

Discovery of rich placers in Last Chance Gulch, Montana; placers were also located at Butte.

Discovery of the Yellow Jacket-Kentuck-Crown Point and Belcher bonanzas in the Comstock lode.

1865: Establishment of the Latin Union, consisting of France, Italy, Switzerland, and Belgium, providing for a double monetary standard at a ratio of 15½ to 1, the agreement to hold good until 1880.

Discovery of the silver lodes at Phillipsburg, Deer Lodge County, Montana, but it was not until 1881 that the great Granite Mountain mine began to develop into a bonanza.

Discovery of the Chollar-Potosi bonanza in the Comstock lode.

1866: Italy suspended specie payments.

Discovery of the Overman-Segregated Belcher-Caledonia and Hale & Norcross bonanzas in the Comstock lode.

Discovery of the famous El Callao mine, Yuruari district, Venezuela.

1867: First international monetary conference convened in Paris by the French Government, at which twenty nations, comprising all the important countries of Europe and America, were represented.

Discovery of rich deposits of silver ore at White Pine, Nev.; these were the first large bodies of silver ore found in a limestone formation in the United States, and the information gained from them led directly to the discovery of the silver-lead deposits of Eureka soon afterwards.

The smelting works of the Boston & Colorado Smelting Company were established at Black Hawk, Colorado; this was an important step for the development of the mines of Gilpin County and other districts in Colorado.

Discovery of the Thames gold-field on the north island of New Zealand.

1868: Greece joined the Latin Union.

Discovery of gold in Western Australia, but it was not until 1887 that any diggings of importance were found.

The Emma silver mine, Little Cottonwood, Utah, was located in August of this year, but no large shipments were made until July, 1870.

Discovery of the Sierra Nevada bonanza in the Comstock lode.

1869: Discovery of the important silver-lead deposits of Eureka, Nevada. The American practice of lead smelting has been developed chiefly from the methods adopted in this district.

The Pacific Railway was completed, and prospecting along its line was greatly stimulated.

The Sutro tunnel to open the Comstock lode was commenced Oct. 19.

Discovery of promising deposits of silver ore at Pioche, Nev.

Copper-silver ore was discovered at Butte, Montana, and a smelting furnace erected at the Parrott mine.

1870: Great silver deposits were discovered at Caracoles, about 120 miles inland in the desert province of Atacama, Chile, on the Bolivian frontier.

The silver mines of Eureka and Pioche, Nevada, became large producers.

1871: The German Empire, by Act of Dec. 4, assumed the sovereign right of coinage and adopted the gold standard; the mintage of silver was discontinued.

Discovery of the great Crown Point-Belcher bonanza in the Comstock lode.

The mines of Big and Little Cottonwood, Utah, made large shipments.

1872: Discovery of silver at Georgetown, New Mexico.

The Ontario vein (silver), Park City, Utah, was located June 19.

1873: The United States, by Act of Congress, Feb. 12, discontinued the coinage of silver dollars. This Act did not demonetize silver in words, although it did so in effect. The silver dollar is not named in it. Precisely what the Act did was to authorize the coinage of silver half-dollars, quarter-dollars, and dimes below standard weight, and of a new silver coin for Asiatic commerce, of standard weight, to be called the "trade dollar," and to prohibit these coins from being legal tender for more than five dollars in any one payment.

Discovery of the "Big Bonanza" in the Consolidated California & Virginia mines on the Comstock lode.

The German Government, by Act of July 9, provided for the retirement of its silver coins and the sale of the bullion.

By a Treasury order, Sept. 6, France limited the amount of silver to be accepted by its mint.

1874: A year of great excitement on the Comstock, the "Big Bonanza" beginning to yield largely, while another bonanza was discovered in the Ophir mine.

Silver was demonetized by the Scandinavian States.

Discovery of promising silver mines, including the Silver King, in the Pinal Range, Arizona.

Early in the year argentiferous lead-carbonate ore was found on Iron Hill, Leadville, and the Lime and Rock claims were located.

By an agreement made in January of this year, the Latin Union was to limit the coinage of silver, exclusive of subsidiary coins, to the following sums for three years: 1874, 140,000,000 francs; 1875, 150,000,000 francs; 1876, 108,000,000 francs. Any nation in the Union had the right to decline coining its quota of this amount any year.

1875: Holland, by Act of June 6, suspended mintage of silver for private account, and established gold coinage with unlimited legal-tender functions, with a ratio of 15.604 to 1; this was a provisional law, to last only until Jan. 1, 1877.

Switzerland declined to coin its quota of silver assigned by the agreement of the Latin Union.

1876: First shipments of silver-lead ore from Leadville, Colo.

Discovery of silver-lead ore at Frisco, Utah, and the Horn Silver mine was opened this year.

In July was brought the first suit of the farmers in California against hydraulic miners, and from this time the débris question became a burning subject of discussion.

The gold-fields of Black Hills, Dakota, began to attract much attention.

Discovery of the Drumlummon ledge (gold) at Marysville, Mont.

Belgium suspended the coinage of silver.

France discontinued the mintage of silver, except for subsidiary coins, until January, 1878, by proclamation of the President, in accordance with the Act of August 5, 1876.

A royal decree was issued in Spain interdicting the coinage of silver except on Government account, and declaring it to be the intention of the Government to limit the legal-tender function of silver to 150 pesetas (about $30) after it had obtained a sufficient amount of gold to make this step practicable.

Russia suspended the coinage of silver for individuals, excepting the amount of silver money needed for trade with China.

By Act of Congress of the United States, August 15, a silver commission was created which reported on March 2, 1877.

1877: Discovery of rich silver veins at Silver Cliff, Colorado, including the Bassick and Bull-Domingo mines.

The curious argentiferous sandstone deposits of Silver Reef, Washington

County, Utah, had been known since 1871 and a mining district was organized there in 1874, but the mines did not commence to produce until 1876.

1878: On Feb. 28, the Congress of the United States passed an Act ordaining the coinage ($2,000,000 per month at least, $4,000,000 at most) on Government account of silver dollars of 412½ grains, 900 fine, and made them full legal tender except where expressly stipulated otherwise by contract.

An international monetary conference was held in August at Paris.

Great excitement at Leadville, Colo., where many new discoveries were made.

The first locations at Tombstone, Ariz., were filed, and the next year the mines (silver) there commenced to produce largely.

Discovery of the silver-lead deposits of Sierra Mojada, Coahuila, Mexico.

1879: The German Government discontinued its sales of silver on May 16.

Resumption of specie payments by the United States.

Discovery of promising veins of silver ore at Aspen, Colo., and in the San Juan region in the southwestern part of the same State.

1880: Reported existence of promising gold veins in the Colar fields of Mysore, Southern India, which were subsequently opened and became large producers.

1881: Discovery of silver ore at Lake Valley, New Mexico.

First important discoveries of silver ore in the Calico district, California.

1882: Decision of the courts prohibiting hydraulic mining in the valleys of navigable rivers of California.

1883: The Mount Morgan gold mine, at Rockhampton, Queensland, began to produce.

The Broken Hill mine (silver-lead) in New South Wales, Australia, was discovered in September.

1884: Discovery of gold in De Kaap district of the Transvaal, South Africa.

1885: Discovery of the silver-lead deposits of the Cœur d'Alene region, Idaho.

The first important discoveries in the " banket " formation, Witwatersrand, Transvaal, South Africa, were made during this year, but active operations were not commenced until 1887.

1890: Act of Congress, July 14, repealing the law of 1878 and providing for the purchase of 4,500,000 ounces of silver monthly, against which certificates are issued, redeemable in either gold or silver.

Establishment of the silver-lead smelting industry in Mexico.

1891: The gold-fields of Mashonaland, South Africa, began to attract attention.

Large exports of gold from New York and purchases by Russia.

Discovery of silver ore at Creede, Colo., and gold at Cripple Creek, in the same State.

1892: The price of silver reached 82 cents per oz., the lowest point ever recorded.

Austro-Hungary adopted the gold monetary standard.

Third international monetary conference held in Brussels on invitation of the United States, adjourning in December without result.

At the close of the year large exports of gold from the United States, causing a very unsettled feeling in financial affairs.

INDEX.

www.ingramcontent.com/pod-product-compliance
Lightning Source LLC
Chambersburg PA
CBHW022025080426
42733CB00007B/733